SHADOW COMMANDER

SHADOW COMMANDER

THE EPIC STORY OF
DONALD D. BLACKBURN
GUERRILLA LEADER &
SPECIAL FORCES HERO

MIKE GUARDIA

CASEMATE
Philadelphia & Newbury

Published in the United States of America and Great Britain in 2011 by
CASEMATE PUBLISHERS
908 Darby Road, Havertown, PA 19083
and
17 Cheap Street, Newbury RG14 5DD

ISBN 978-1-61200-065-7
Digital Edition: ISBN 978-1-61200-079-4

Cataloging-in-publication data is available from the Library of Congress
and the British Library.

10 9 8 7 6 5 4 3 2 1

Printed and bound in the United States of America.

For a complete list of Casemate titles please contact:

CASEMATE PUBLISHERS (US)
Telephone (610) 853-9131, Fax (610) 853-9146
E-mail: casemate@casematepublishing.com

CASEMATE PUBLISHERS (UK)
Telephone (01635) 231091, Fax (01635) 41619
E-mail: casemate-uk@casematepublishing.co.uk

CONTENTS

INTRODUCTION

T he fires on Bataan burned with a primitive fury on the evening of
April 9, 1942, illuminating the white flags of surrender against the
nighttime sky. Woefully outnumbered, outgunned, and ill-equipped, the
battered remnants of the American-Philippine army surrendered to the
wrath of the Rising Sun. Yet amongst the chaos and devastation of the
American defeat, Army Captain Donald D. Blackburn refused to lay
down his arms.

Together with Russell Volckmann, the pair escaped from Bataan
and fled to the mountainous jungles of North Luzon, where they raised
a private army of over 22,000 men against the Japanese. Under Volckmann's leadership, Blackburn organized a guerrilla regiment from
among the native tribes in the Cagayan Valley. "Blackburn's Headhunters," as they came to be known, devastated the Japanese 14th Army
within the eastern provinces of North Luzon and destroyed the Japanese naval base at Aparri—the largest enemy anchorage in the Philippine
Islands.

After the war, Blackburn remained on active duty and played a
key role in initiating Special Forces operations in Southeast Asia. In
1959, as commander of the 77th Special Forces Group, he spearheaded
Operation *White Star*—the first major deployment of American Special
Forces to a country with an active insurgency. Six years later, at the
outset of America's combat mission in Vietnam, Blackburn took over
the highly classified Studies and Observations Group (SOG).

In the wake of the CIA's disastrous *Leaping Lena* reconnaissance program, Blackburn revitalized the special operations campaign in South Vietnam. Sending cross-border reconnaissance teams into Laos, he discovered the clandestine networks and supply nodes of the infamous Ho Chi Minh Trail. Taking this information directly to General Westmoreland, Blackburn received authorization to conduct full-scale operations against the NVA and Viet Cong operating along the Ho Chi Minh Trail.

Following his return to the United States, Blackburn was appointed "Special Assistant for Counterinsurgency and Special Activities," where he was the architect of the famous Son Tay Prison Raid. Officially termed Operation *Ivory Coast* (and later, *Kingpin*) the Son Tay Raid was the largest POW rescue mission—and indeed, the largest Special Forces operation—of the Vietnam War.

The idea for this project began in January 2008 when I was conducting research for my first book, *American Guerrilla: The Forgotten Heroics of Russell W. Volckmann*. In the opening stages of the war, Blackburn and Volckmann developed a close friendship while they were assigned to Headquarters Staff, 11th Division (Philippine Army). Previously, I knew nothing about Donald Blackburn outside of Volckmann's literature. However, at the US Army's Military History Institute (MHI) in Carlisle Barracks, Pennsylvania, I discovered the 400-page transcript of an interview conducted with Blackburn by Lieutenant Colonel Robert Smith (USAF) in 1983. As part of the "Senior Officers Oral History Program," this interview covered nearly every aspect of Blackburn's life—his childhood, the Philippines, Vietnam, Son Tay, and his activities since retirement. After reading the transcript, I was surprised that, despite his impressive career, no one had ever written a biography of Donald Blackburn.

At this stage in my research, I assumed that Blackburn, like many of Volckmann's comrades, had passed away. However, the interview transcript included a bio-data section indicating that Blackburn had two children, Donald Jr. and Susan. I initiated a public records search to locate Blackburn's children and, in the course of doing so, was surprised to discover that Blackburn himself was still alive and living in Sarasota, Florida. Contacting Blackburn's family, I secured a visitation in March 2008.

Unfortunately, Blackburn had been suffering from Alzheimer's which diluted much of his memory. However, his daughter, Susan, granted me access to all of his records. Comprising nearly two whole filing cabinets, "The Donald D. Blackburn Collection" included a wealth of photographs, letters, war trophies, guerrilla reports, and official duplicates of government documents. I also learned that Blackburn, like Volckmann, had kept a diary while in the Philippines. The diary spanned the period from October 23, 1941 to April 29, 1944. Although Blackburn's diary contained fewer entries than Volckmann's, Blackburn often wrote his entries at greater length.

Blackburn's diary became the basis of the 1955 book, *Blackburn's Headhunters*. The idea for that work began in 1950, when Blackburn was teaching at West Point in the Department of Military Psychology and Leadership. As it were, Blackburn's wartime experience caught the attention of the Commandant of Cadets, then-Major General Paul D. Harkins. Convincing Blackburn to get his story published, General Harkins tasked his younger brother, Philip Harkins, to pen *Blackburn's Headhunters*.*

Four years after its publication, Hollywood turned *Blackburn's Headhunters* into a feature film. Allied Artists, a prominent B-movie studio, began production in 1958 and invited Blackburn to serve as a technical advisor on the film. Actor Keith Andes (a Broadway baritone and former leading man to Marilyn Monroe) portrayed Blackburn in the film. Under the new title *Surrender—Hell!*, the movie was released on July 26, 1959. The film was a modest success at the box office, but Blackburn hated it. He thought that the filmmakers had taken too much artistic license by creating subplots that never existed. On one occasion, he called it "the worst movie I've ever seen." Modern critics have often referred to it as typical 1950s B-movie fare.

In Spring 2008, *Surrender—Hell!* had not yet been released on any home video format. Determined to see whether the film held any research value, I began searching for the rights-holder. Allied Artists had since gone out of business and its film library had been acquired by Republic Pictures. However, my search for *Surrender—Hell!* ulti-

---

*General Harkins went on to become the inaugural commander of the Military Assistance Command—Vietnam (MACV) in 1962. The younger Harkins was an accomplished writer whose other titles included *Road Race* and *Breakaway Back*.

mately led me to a gentlemen named Kit Parker, proprietor of Kit Parker Films International. Parker's film studio specializes in restoring old *noir* films and re-releases them through VCI Entertainment. Contacting Parker about the rights to *Surrender—Hell!*, he informed me that his production team had restored the film and were planning to re-release it on DVD that summer. After watching *Surrender—Hell!* I can understand Blackburn's frustration with the subplots and historical inaccuracies. And although it provided no help to my research, I still found it to be an enjoyable film.

Blackburn also conducted interviews with the Special Warfare Center in 1988 and 1993, respectively. Both interviews cover the same topics as the 1983 MHI Oral History Project. The transcript for the 1988 interview currently rests at the US Special Operations Command History Office at Fort Bragg, North Carolina. The audiotapes for the 1993 interview are also at Fort Bragg, filed in the JFK Special Warfare Center and School Archives.

Works produced by Blackburn's own hand include "War Within a War: The Philippines, 1942–1945" and "Operations of the 11th Infantry, USAFIP-NL, in the Capture of Mayoyao, Mountain Province, PI, 26 July–8 August 1945." The former is an article Blackburn submitted for the Summer 1988 edition of *Conflict*, while the later was Blackburn's capstone research paper for the Infantry Officers Advanced Course, which he attended in 1947–48. "War Within a War" gives an overview of his and Volckmann's guerrilla campaign in North Luzon. The paper describes in detail Blackburn's own experience as a regimental commander fighting the Japanese in the Mayayao Campaign.

I was fortunate that there were many secondary sources available for this project. These included John Plaster's seminal work, *SOG*, and Harve Saal's massive four-volume treatise *Behind Enemy Lines: SOG—MACV Studies and Observations Group*. Benjamin Schemmer's *The Raid* and John Gargus' *The Son Tay Raid: American POWs in Vietnam Were Not Forgotten* are perhaps the two most authoritative works on the Son Tay Raid. Other references for this project included the *US Army in Vietnam* series and *Vietnam Studies* series produced by the US Army Center for Military History.

As with any sources, however, none of them are without their potential liabilities. Volckmann and Blackburn achieved remarkable consistency with their respective diaries. However, there are a few discrepancies. Names and places are often spelled differently. Blackburn describes meeting people who Volckmann never mentions. In some instances, the chronology of events is different. For instance, Volckmann records one event happening on a Wednesday, while Blackburn recalls the same incident happening on a Friday. Those who have read *American Guerrilla* may notice that some of these discrepancies are evidenced in *Shadow Commander*. However, this is only because I am telling the story from Blackburn's perspective.

Blackburn's Headhunters, while not a "secondary source" in the strictest sense, may have had some distillation from Philip Harkins. However, in Blackburn's private collection, I found many letters to and from Harkins. In Harkins' correspondence, he often asked Blackburn for clarification on diary entries he didn't understand or verification of characters and locales. This, I believe, indicates that Harkins wanted to retain the integrity of Blackburn's story.

Blackburn's interviews from 1983, 1988, and 1993 were conducted years after he retired from the military. As with any event that happened long ago, memory often distorts and rearranges the facts of the story. However, during these years, Blackburn still had his mental faculties and possessed remarkable memory. Furthermore, these interviews do not greatly contradict one another nor the events told in *Blackburn's Headhunters*. * Aside from Blackburn himself, who was tragically losing his fight against Alzheimer's, the other subjects who I interviewed for this project were all of sound mind and consistent with their recollections. In sum, I believe that my research and selection of source material warrant the credibility to support the information in this book.

This book is, first and foremost, a biography of Donald Blackburn. His life is the driving force behind the narrative; therefore, the reader will not find any detailed discussions on the larger topics of the secret war in Laos or the Son Tay Raid. Blackburn's life touched upon many historical events, and while I have provided some detail and background about these events for the sake of context, these topics are discussed only inasmuch as Blackburn participated in them.

---

*The quotations found in this book are from either Blackburn's interviews or *Blackburn's Headhunters* unless otherwise noted.

I give special thanks to Donald Blackburn, Jr., Susan Blackburn Douglas, and her husband, Bill Douglas, for their kindness and hospitality throughout this project. Without their support, this book may never have been written. I would also like to thank the courteous and attentive staff at the National Archives and Records Administration, the Military History Institute, The Special Warfare Center History Support Office, and the Copyright Clearance Center, for their assistance during my research. My appreciaton also goes to the Army Center for Military History, whose maps provided the basis of information for those which appear in this work. Finally, I would like to thank the editorial/production team at Casemate Publishers for the patience and professional support they provided throughout every phase of this project.

In a career that spanned over thirty years, Donald D. Blackburn was a true hero of the Army Special Forces. *Shadow Commander* is his story.

CHAPTER 1

CALL OF DUTY

The morning sun beat down mercilessly on what little remained of Headquarters Battalion, 12th Infantry, and its commander, First Lieutenant Donald D. Blackburn, knew that time was running out. Crouching behind their hastily dug-in fighting positions, his young Filipinos—inaugural members of the Philippine Army—prepared to open fire on the Japanese landing craft barreling towards the shore. The enemy had been probing their coastal defenses for the past twelve hours, determined to crush the "speed bump" that lay between them and their conquest of the Philippine Islands. As he braced himself for the incoming wave of enemy troops, Blackburn began to wonder how he had gotten himself into this mess, or if he would ever live to tell about it.

The story of Donald Dunwoody Blackburn begins on the idyllic shores of the American Sunbelt. Born on September 14, 1916 in West Palm Beach, Florida, "Don" spent his formative years growing up in the suburbs of Tampa. He never revealed much about his upbringing, other than to say that it was typical of most boys growing up in western Florida. Indeed, the young man dedicated most of his childhood to swimming, sailing, and other nautical pursuits. In many ways, Don Blackburn was also a product of his time—his was the generation raised on the harrowing tales of the Great War, the decadence of the Roaring Twenties, and the bitter hardships of the Great Depression. And, like

The earliest known photographs of Donald Blackburn: (left) in 1918, (right) 1920. The Donald D. Blackburn Collection

Donald Blackburn's first grade class, 1923. Blackburn stands in the middle of the second row, just above the girl in the hat. The Donald D. Blackburn Collection

many young men of his day, he was fervently patriotic. From an early age he admired the sense of duty and patriotism that came with military service. Despite his childhood interest in waterborne activities, Don found himself attracted to the culture and lifestyle of the United States Army.

Graduating from Plant High School in 1934, Blackburn announced his decision to enroll in an Army ROTC program. That fall he matriculated at the University of Florida, pursuing a degree in Business with a minor in Military Science. He enjoyed college life, but admitted that "I squeaked by through the skin of my teeth . . . I just wasn't motivated towards anything in particular, other than enjoying fraternity life." Nevertheless, his experiences as an Army cadet validated the passions he had had for soldiering. Excelling in many areas of his cadetship, Don was an active member in the Scabbard & Blade Society, and rose to the rank of Cadet Captain. After serving as an ROTC Company Commander during his senior year, Blackburn graduated in 1938 with a commission as a Second Lieutenant of Infantry.

Although he was an outstanding cadet, the Thompson Act of 1932 ultimately prevented Don from serving on active duty. A hallmark of an isolationist Congress, the Thompson Act limited the number of ROTC graduates who could enter active duty within a certain fiscal year. Unwittingly cast into the Army Reserve, Blackburn decided to make the best of it and begin searching for a full-time job.

Above: *Donald Blackburn, 1926.*
Below: *Senior photo,*
Plant High School, 1934.
The Donald D. Blackburn Collection

As it was throughout most of the Depression Era, the best job opportunities were in the public sector. Coincidentally, Blackburn's uncle—a pioneer of early avionics—landed him a job with the Civil Aeronautics Board (CAB) in Washington, DC. This job placement was fortuitous as it reunited Don with his former ROTC instructor, Lieutenant Colonel Claude Adams. Adams had just been transferred to the office of the Army Chief of Staff, only a few blocks away from the CAB offices. One summer night in 1940, while enjoying dinner at Adams' house, Don confessed that although he enjoyed his job at the Aeronautics Board, he regretted not being able to serve on active duty. Hearing this, Adams stopped him and said, "Well, Don, why don't you do it? Your name, in all probability, will come up for call to active duty this year [1940]."

Shortly before Congress passed the Selective Training and Service Act (the first peacetime draft in American history), the Army had begun calling its Reserve officers into active service for a period of one year—renewable based on national security and manpower needs. Adams, however, cautioned Blackburn, saying that "If your name comes up this year, you're going to have to drop out of school." Blackburn had been attending night classes at Georgetown University Law School and, ideally, was to sit for the DC Bar Exam in less than a year. Nevertheless, he looked Adams straight in the eye and said, "I'd just as soon go on active duty."

Blackburn (back row, far left) as a new member of Sigma Alpha Epsilon— *University of Florida chapter, 1934.* The Donald D. Blackburn Collection

Blackburn and friends at a college house party, 1936. Said Blackburn of his college days, "I just wasn't motivated towards anything in particular, other than enjoying fraternity life." The Donald D. Blackburn Collection

In all, Blackburn had no reason to fear being left out of active service, for the political climate of 1940 was vastly different from what it had been only two years earlier. Isolationism still rang high in halls of Congress, but the ideology was quickly losing steam as Nazi Germany—which had inaugurated another European war on September 1, 1939—advanced on all fronts. For the first time in nearly a quarter-century, the U.S. government authorized a full-scale increase in military spending. Meanwhile, across the pond, the British relied heavily on American logistics in their life-and-death struggle against the *Luftwaffe* and the *Kriegsmarine*. Still, many Americans hoped that the war in Europe would run its course without their involvement. The Empire of Japan, at this stage, was of little concern to anyone. Despite its recent aggressions on the Chinese mainland, everyone knew that the Rising Sun would *never* challenge the U.S. Navy.

In his conversation with Adams, Blackburn expressed a desire to go to Fort Benning, Georgia—the "Home of the Infantry." According to Blackburn, "It so happened that General Embrick, the CG [Commanding General] of the IV Corps Area located in Atlanta, was in town. Since Adams was in the Chief's Office, he talked to Embrick and it was arranged that in September—this was then August of 1940—I would receive orders to go to Fort Benning," orders which assigned him to the 24th Infantry Regiment.

*Graduation portrait from the
University of Florida, 1938.*
The Donald D. Blackburn Collection

Assuming his role as a now-active duty lieutenant, Blackburn was sent to the Communications School on-post and was appointed as a Battalion Signal Officer. For the first few months at Fort Benning, Don lived the life of a typical bachelor until one night (at a local dance) when he won the affections of a young lady named Ann Smith. The young belle was introduced to him as the girlfriend of one of his former classmates from the University of Florida. But Blackburn, smitten as he was, pursued the young woman until she finally relented. They began dating in November 1940 and by the following summer they had set their marriage date for September 1941. Destiny, however, was about to throw them a curveball.

After returning home from maneuvers in Louisiana, Blackburn discovered that his active duty tour had been extended. He wasn't surprised. In fact, he had seen it coming. As the situation in Europe deteriorated—along with continuing tension in Asia—there was hardly a Reservist whose tour *hadn't* been extended. But shortly afterward, Blackburn recalled that "a notice appeared on the regimental bulletin board asking for volunteers for the Philippines." He didn't think about it again until the next day, when Second Lieutenant Harry Kuykendall barged into his tent and asked, "Did you see that?"

"Yes," Blackburn grumbled.

"Did you volunteer?" Harry asked him.

"Hell no!"

"Neither did I, but I know they're going to volunteer me."

"What makes you think so?" Blackburn said.

"It's just fate."

Unfortunately, fate cast a grim shadow on Don Blackburn that day,

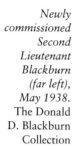

Newly commissioned Second Lieutenant Blackburn (far left), May 1938. The Donald D. Blackburn Collection

as the next morning he discovered that his name (right alongside Kuykendall's) was on the list of new officers reassigned to the Philippine Islands.

Blackburn was not amused; he couldn't go to the Philippines, he was getting married. "And I hardly knew where the Philippines were," he added. Phoning Lieutenant Colonel Adams to tell him the news, Blackburn was surprised when Adams congratulated him on the new posting. An assignment to the Philippine Islands was every soldier's dream, Adams said. Tropical beaches, warm weather, and the "Pearl of the Orient"—*he should be so lucky.* And "if anything's going to happen," he told Blackburn, "it's going to happen in Europe, and not in the Philippines." Be that as it may, Blackburn still had a fiancée. What would this do to his marriage plans?

Blackburn's identification photograph taken at Fort Benning upon his assignment to the 24th Infantry Regiment. The Donald D. Blackburn Collection

Consulting with Ann later that night, Don told her, "You're going to have to hang in there, because I'm not going to marry you with me over there and you over here." He never mentioned the details of her reaction, but suffice to say that Ann "didn't think it was such a hot arrangement." All things considered, however, Don knew it was for best. He loved her dearly, but until the situation overseas could be resolved, he simply wouldn't take the risk of making her a widow so early into her marriage. Sooner or later, he said, Americans would be in this war whether they liked it or not.

An American Commonwealth since the Spanish-American War in 1898, the Philippines were in the midst of their transition to full sovereignty. In 1935, Congress had passed the Tydings-McDuffie Act, which set a ten-year timeline for Philippine independence and made provisions for establishing a new Philippine Army. To fill the ranks of this inaugural army, Philippine President Manuel Quezon drew personnel from the US Philippine Scouts and the Philippine Constabulary. The Philippine Scouts were a highly trained and well-equipped American Army unit in which all of the enlisted men (and most of the junior officers) were Filipino. The Philippine Constabulary was the national police force.

American forces in the Philippines fell under the jurisdiction of the United States Armed Forces—Far East (USAFFE).* Commanded by an Army General (at the time, Douglas MacArthur), USAFFE encompassed all American ground forces, the Asiatic Fleet, the Far East Air Force, and the semi-autonomous Philippine Army. USAFFE's mission was to defend the archipelago and to train the new Philippine Army. To this end, the US Army sent thousands of its young officers to the Pacific to serve as low-level commanders and instructors in the Philippine Army.

With his orders in hand, Blackburn departed Washington, DC on a train bound for San Francisco. The trip was quite an odyssey as most of the passengers were military personnel, and nearly all of them were headed to the Philippines. On arrival in Lake Charles, Louisiana, the train was boarded by a group of soldiers just in from maneuvers outside Camp Polk. From there, the trip took a rather interesting turn. In the tradition of easily bored young men, the new GIs invented outlandish ways to keep themselves entertained. Shortly after crossing into Texas, one fellow proclaimed, "Let's have a party . . . I can't stand this thing." With that, he went rummaging through the baggage car and

---

*Pronounced: "you-saw-fee."

Blackburn at Fort Benning, 1941, on the eve of his departure to the Philippine Islands. The Donald D. Blackburn Collection

produced a banjo, some exotic booze, and a handful of hula skirts. Blackburn stood there in bewilderment as the young man proceeded to coax the few women on board to put on the hula skirts and start dancing. Booze and good tidings made their way around the passenger car as the train lumbered westward to California.

Arriving in San Francisco, however, the mood was decidedly different. The once joyful lot now somberly boarded the USS *Holbrook* en route to the Philippines. As it were, the passenger manifest included none other than the "barracks fortune-teller," Harry Kuykendall. Over the twenty-three day voyage, Kuykendall, once again, was up to his fatalistic fortune-telling. One day, in the ship's galley, Blackburn came upon "Old Harry" and found him reading a copy of *Orphans of the Pacific* by John Michener. Kuykendall said, "I've just been reading about these stinking barrios and all the disease over there, and I can see now that when I get there, I'm going to be put in one of these barrios and get some kind of tropical disease."

When the *Holbrook* finally arrived in the Philippines, Don told him, "Now Kuykendall, you read the good things in that book, because I'm not going to the awful places you've read about." Trying to inject a little bit of optimism into the somber fellow, Blackburn speculated that they might end up in Baguio together. Baguio, a city nestled within the mountains of the *Cordillera Central*, was home to Camp John Hay, one of the nicest military bases in the archipelago. Disembarking from the ship, the assignment orders were read aloud and the pair discovered that they were, in fact, assigned to Baguio. "See?" Blackburn told him, "I knew it—'Lieutenant Kuykendall, Baguio'."

"Oh it won't last," Kuykendall interjected. "I'll end up in the stinking damn malaria-ridden country."

Blackburn tried to remain upbeat. Perhaps this year-long tour in the Philippines would pass without incident.

CHAPTER 2

OFF TO THE PHILIPPINES

A fter being fitted for nearly a dozen tropical uniforms, and sifting through the endless volumes of paperwork, Blackburn received his orders to the 12th Infantry at Camp Holmes just outside Baguio—about 175 miles north of Manila and nearly 4,000 feet above sea level. The regiment was one of four that belonged to the 11th Division (Philippine Army).

Arriving at Camp Holmes on October 23, 1941, Blackburn reported to Major Martin Moses, the Regimental Commander. Moses was an Infantry officer and a West Point graduate—Class of 1929. He had been in the Philippines for quite some time and had just earned his eligibility for promotion to Lieutenant Colonel. Rather short and slight of build, Moses' reputation belied his appearance—he was stern, direct, and spoke with the vigor of a man twice his size. He was polite, but not friendly. Reviewing Blackburn's orders, Moses gave him a look and said "Ok Don, you'll be an instructor for us."

"Instructing what, sir?"

"Communications and motor transport." Blackburn had a working familiarity with both subjects, so the job sounded all right. But what Moses neglected to tell him was that the battalion had no trucks, no radios, and no field manuals for either topic.

Early that afternoon, Blackburn arrived at the Headquarters Battalion to meet his new charges. The reception, however, was hardly enjoyable. Looking at the state of his men, Blackburn discovered that

A 1940 postcard depicting the Army-Navy Club in Manila.
The Donald D. Blackburn Collection

the Philippine Army was an "army" that existed only on paper. His young soldiers—most of them conscripts—were members of the Ilocano tribe. They were a strong and healthy bunch, but nearly half of them were barefooted—no money had been allocated for shoes. And what little equipment they did have were military hand-me-downs from the First World War. On his person, the Filipino soldier carried little more than a summer uniform, canteen, and rifle. The rifles, however, were Enfields—old British-model guns that hadn't been fired since the Treaty of Versailles. At first, he could hardly fathom it—the U.S. had been working on the Philippine defense project for the past six years, and *this* was the only progress they had made?

Undaunted by the challenges, Blackburn solicited help from a nearby precinct of the Philippine Constabulary. Borrowing one of their patrol vehicles, Blackburn secured his battalion's first motorized asset. His next stop was the local bus company, owned and operated by Philippine Army reservist Bando Dagwa. "Without much discussion," Blackburn recalled, "Dagwa loaned me a pickup truck" along with instruction booklets on how to operate a motor vehicle. From there, the young Lieutenant Blackburn began making visual mock-ups of a steering column, gearshift, and clutch. Any part of the vehicle that

Postcard of the Officers' Mess at Camp John Hay, where Blackburn was stationed upon his arrival in the Philippines. The back of the postcard is addressed to his parents, Mr. and Mrs. Frank Blackburn, who lived in Washington DC at the time. The Donald D. Blackburn Collection

he couldn't reproduce was drawn on the company blackboard.

Blackburn could deal with his battalion's supply issues. But the soldiers' discipline—or lack thereof—was a different matter altogether. In fact, long before Blackburn's arrival, "discipline" had become somewhat of a joke. In keeping with their tribal tradition, the Ilocanos wore their hair in long, flowing, black locks, well beyond the length of military regulation. To correct the problem, Blackburn armed his officers with scissors, ready to cut off the offensive locks at a moment's notice. The Ilocano officers, however, were laughably incompetent and had little sway over the men they were expected to lead. Since many of the officers would drink, gamble, and gossip with their men, the authoritative relationship had gone out the window.

Gathering the troops for their first round of instruction, however,

Blackburn discovered an even greater problem. Nearly three-quarters of his men couldn't speak English. Aghast and frustrated, Blackburn enlisted the help of any interpreter he could find. But even with his interpreters, the task of instructing these young Filipinos seemed like an exercise in futility. They would laugh, giggle, and stand sleepy-eyed in front of Blackburn's mock-ups. They were so frequently inattentive and disobedient that he would have to curse and threaten them just to force their compliance. To make matters worse, none of the Ilocanos had ever driven a motor vehicle. To stem the tide of their inexperience, however, Blackburn said:

> We jacked the back wheels up so the trainees wouldn't go over the side of the mountain while learning to shift gears. You can imagine trying to get the equivalent of a company trained on one vehicle, and me speaking only English!

Indeed, every day was a battle of wills as Don Blackburn tried to whip his disinterested soldiers into a cohesive unit. But he nonetheless persevered.

Adding insult to injury were Blackburn's living arrangements. He had a nice billet at Camp John Hay (on the other side of Baguio) but the commute into Camp Holmes just added to his frustrations. Camp John Hay was home to the elite Philippine Scouts and, by virtue of being an American outfit, the Scouts were privy to the best equipment in the archipelago. A majority of the Scouts at John Hay were Igorot tribesmen who, like the Ilocanos, were physically fit, but the Igorots were much more disciplined. Blackburn envied the officers who had been assigned to the Philippine Scouts; it always seemed that they had fewer headaches to deal with.

On the morning of December 5th, the 12th Infantry Regiment received orders to vacate its post at Camp Holmes and move into defensive positions outside Umingan in Pangasian province. At first, Don didn't know what to make of it. USAFFE had just finished its last round of maneuvers a few months ago—they couldn't be conducting another training cycle this early, could they? Unbeknownst to Blackburn, however, USAFFE Intelligence had detected a Japanese naval convoy entering the South China Sea.

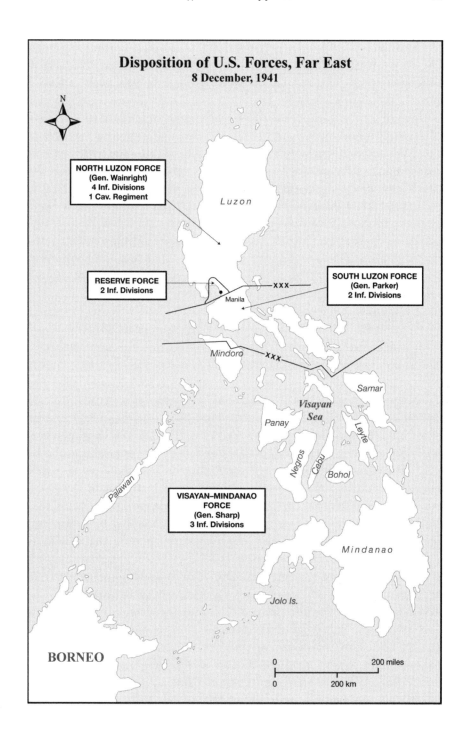

Disposition of U.S. Forces, Far East
8 December, 1941

N

NORTH LUZON FORCE
(Gen. Wainright)
4 Inf. Divisions
1 Cav. Regiment

Luzon

RESERVE FORCE
2 Inf. Divisions

xxx

SOUTH LUZON FORCE
(Gen. Parker)
2 Inf. Divisions

Manila

Mindoro

xxx

Samar

Visayan Sea

Panay

Leyte

Negros

Cebu

Bohol

Palawan

VISAYAN–MINDANAO
FORCE
(Gen. Sharp)
3 Inf. Divisions

Mindanao

Jolo Is.

BORNEO

0   200 miles

0   200 km

The camp at Umingan was a welcome change for Don Blackburn. The move into Pangasian province placed him in the lowlands of Central Luzon, where finely crafted nipa palm huts were built to accommodate the entire Division. At times, Blackburn seemed more like a cattle herder than a leader of troops as he directed his men to their field billets and rallied them for morning muster. Thinking that this was all a training maneuver, he felt eager to get back into the swing of real soldiering. Field exercises and war games were what he lived for. But after three days in the camp, Don would find out that this was no game.

In the early morning hours of December 8, Second Lieutenant Charlie Youngblood, a heavy weapons instructor with Headquarters Battalion, came rushing into the Officers' Mess Hall. Panting, sweating, and visibly shaken, the poor man trembled as he tried to sputter what was obviously bad news. With all eyes fixated on Youngblood, Blackburn rose from his breakfast table to try and calm the man down.

"What is it, Charlie?"

"The Japs just bombed Baguio! They got Pearl Harbor, too!" A hush descended over the Mess Hall. Aside from the few men dropping their utensils to the table in disbelief, there was nothing but dead silence.

Now it all made sense. The move to Umingan hadn't been a training maneuver; USAFFE had been putting itself on a wartime footing. But how could the Japanese have attacked the US? And why Pearl Harbor? Suddenly all the pieces of the puzzle began to fit together. With the US Pacific Fleet devastated at Pearl, the Philippines would have no shield against a pending invasion—the Asiatic Fleet couldn't hold off the Imperial Japanese Navy on its own. The Far East Air Force would take flight to defend the skies over Luzon. But with what? P-40s? The enemy Zeroes would tear them apart. And then there were the American ground units. The Philippine Scouts and American infantry forces could hold their own, but Blackburn knew that they would eventually be overrun. And he didn't even want to think about the slaughter that would ensue when the ill-equipped Philippine Army met the Rising Sun. The other regiments might have better luck, but if they were anything like his undisciplined Ilocanos, USAFFE would be in serious trouble. Balling up his fists in quiet frustration, Blackburn knew the game was over before it had even started. But be that as it may, the Japanese weren't going to get him without a fight. Leaving Charlie Youngblood to regain his composure, Blackburn stormed out of the mess hall with the words of Lieutenant Colonel Adams echoing in his head, "If anything's going to happen, it's going to happen in Europe, and not in the Philippines."

Running out into the morning sunlight, Blackburn discovered the whole camp bustling with chaos over the news. It was an alarming sight. Americans, Filipinos, officers, enlisted men—a virtual sea of bodies running helter-skelter, trying to make sense of the confusion. Ammo crates, boxes, rifles, and crew-served weapons were thrown onto the backs and into the arms of any soldier nearby. Officers barked orders to their men, trying to make themselves heard over the growing noise. Amidst the chaos, Blackburn found Major Moses. "Don, I need you to get back to the battalion area," he said. "Rally the troops, we're moving out."

The order had come to move the regiment about thirty miles west to the Division Headquarters at Manaoag. Although the regiment still had no trucks, Moses commandeered a fleet of commercial buses. Hording his Ilocanos into a bus, Blackburn got behind the wheel and sped away from the camp at Umingan. But after only a few minutes on the road, a loud popping noise burst through the air, and the bus shimmied to a halt. *A tire had blown out.* Pounding his hands on the steering wheel, Blackburn hastened himself off the bus and ordered the Ilocanos to follow. Further down the road, several other buses had encountered similar fates: one bus had run out of gas while another had blown a radiator.

Piling equipment and personnel into the few remaining buses, the regiment looked more like a gypsy caravan than a military convoy by the time it reached Manaoag. Along the way, Don received a rather unexpected promotion.

> He [Major Moses] said to me, 'You take over as the battalion commander, just assume command.' There wasn't any problem because the Filipino commander was damn glad to have someone take over. He didn't know what he was doing, anyway. All of a sudden, my battalion lost its identity as a technical unit; with every man having a rifle, we became a rifle battalion.

As a young lieutenant with less than two years of active service, Don

Blackburn was now a battalion commander. Looking at the state of his Ilocanos, though, he didn't know whether to be proud or terrified.

On the night of December 11, 1941—Blackburn's first night as commander—Headquarters Battalion was ordered to move up the coast of the China Sea to Damortis. This time, however, the move would be done by railcar, a welcome relief after the debacle of the tour buses. Two days earlier, the first elements of the Japanese 14th Army had landed at Aparri on the northern coast of Luzon, while another contingent landed at Vigan, about eighty miles north of Manaoag.

Blackburn's train arrived in Damortis shortly after midnight. His orders were to defend the beach and the roads leading into town. The Japanese expeditionary force that landed at Vigan had begun moving south, and Major Moses had selected Damortis to be the site of initial contact. Emplacing a few rifle platoons along the beach—supported by mortars and heavy machine guns on the hills behind the railroad—Blackburn was satisfied with the night's cantonment.

But as he was directing the last of his companies from the train station, a sudden burst of fire came from the beach. Startled, Blackburn and the other Ilocanos in the station hit the floor. Without warning, the rifle platoons on the beach had opened fire. They were soon joined by the machine gunners and mortar crews who began lobbing rounds into the surf.

Blackburn was incredulous. "What the hell are they shooting at?" he wondered.

But then, almost as soon as it had started, the firing stopped. Scrambling to his feet, Blackburn ran out the station door and onto the beach. Approaching one of the rifle company's foxholes, a nervous Ilocano reported to him, in broken English, "Something in the sea, please sir." Blackburn gazed into the abyss but saw nothing to indicate the wake of a ship or any landing craft. It was nothing, Blackburn told himself. Just their imaginations.

As if the night hadn't been stressful enough, Major Moses ordered the battalion to pack up again and move to Bauang, two hours north. Arriving at Bauang on the morning of December 13, Blackburn's new orders were to defend the town along Highway 3 running north to south and the Nagulian Road running east towards Baguio. Bauang, it seemed, was a better place to defend than Damortis. If the Japanese

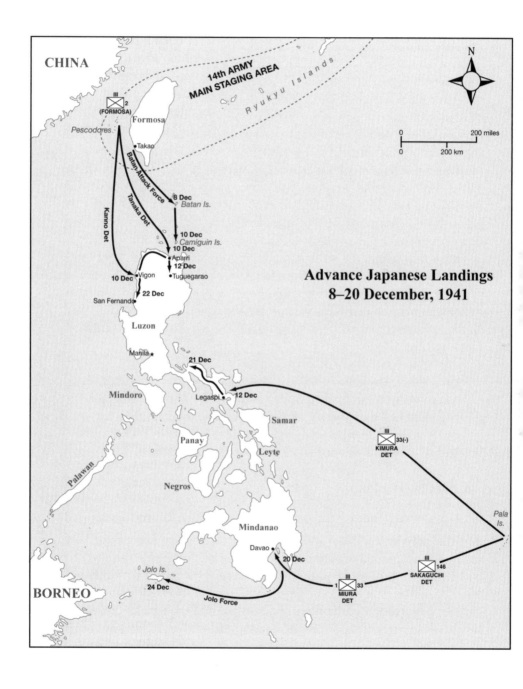

CHINA

14th ARMY
MAIN STAGING AREA

R y u k y u   I s l a n d s

N

2
(FORMOSA)

Pescadores

Formosa

•Takao

0   200 miles
0   200 km

Batan Attack Force

Tanaka Det

Kanno Det

8 Dec
Batan Is.

10 Dec
Camiguin Is.
10 Dec
•Aparri
12 Dec
10 Dec •Vigon •Tuguegarao
22 Dec
San Fernando•

**Advance Japanese Landings
8–20 December, 1941**

Luzon

Manila ★

21 Dec

Mindoro

Legaspi• 12 Dec

Samar

Panay

Leyte

33(-)
KIMURA
DET

Palawan

Negros

Mindanao

*Pala
Is.*

Davao •
20 Dec

146
SAKAGUCHI
DET

Jolo Is.

24 Dec

BORNEO

Jolo Force

1   33
MIURA
DET

were still headed south from Vigan, they would have to use Highway 3 to get to Bataan or Manila. That route would send them into Bauang where, canalized by the China Sea on the left, and the Cordillera Central on the right, they would become easy targets for the USAFFE defenders.

After Blackburn had set up his headquarters in a local schoolhouse, he made several reconnaissance trips to the Division's Outpost Line of Resistance near San Juan, about twenty miles north of Bauang. The San Juan Line was defended by the 13th Infantry under the command of Major Arthur Noble, a West Point classmate of Moses. Whereas Major Moses was stern and serious, Art Noble was a delightfully charming fellow. The two had been friends for years and it was obvious that Noble had a disarming effect on his comrade, for Moses would suddenly lose his deadpan veneer in the presence of his friend.

Back at Bauang, the week passed without enemy contact, but there were plenty of warning signs from the "fifth column." One day, a pair of drunken civilians were picked up along the Nagulian Road. One was a Japanese man named Hikawa, and the other was an American named Speth, who claimed to be a veteran of the Spanish-American War. Blackburn recalled:

> I arrested them at Bauang, and took them into the schoolhouse where we had established our headquarters. They had a black bag just filled with money, and the story that was that they were going to try and work out a deal with the Japanese, who had landed north of us, not to destroy or damage Baguio. I don't know how they figured they would buy the Japs off, but that's what I was told.

Later that week, Blackburn received a call from a civilian lookout: a fishing trawler had been spotted off the coast of San Fernando. Normally, a fishing vessel would have been no cause for alarm, but this one was flying the Japanese ensign. Blackburn sent the report to higher ups and requested that the regimental artillery be brought forward to engage. Unfortunately, the report languished and the trawler continued south, appearing off the shores of Bauang early the following morning. The vessel was obviously a naval spy vessel trying to get a sense of what Allied units were defending the coast. Don was about to order his men to fire on the trawler when he suddenly realized that it was too far out range for even the best of his small arms. Thus, in bitter frustration, he watched helplessly as the enemy trawler sailed away.

These passive interludes, however, came to an end on the 21st of December. The Japanese made contact with Noble's regiment at the Outpost Line of Resistance. To help his old friend, Moses decided to cannibalize Blackburn's battalion and send its rifle companies northward to assist Noble. This move, however, left Blackburn with no vehicles, no radios, no mortars, and only one rifle company.

How was he supposed to defend Bauang with only *one* company?

Among those who stayed behind with Blackburn were Lieutenants Shelby Newman and Charlie Youngblood, the frightened young man who had first delivered the news of Pearl Harbor. Gathering the two Lieutenants underneath a palm tree, Blackburn laid out his strategy. He reminded them of the Japanese trawler from earlier in the day. If that trawler had made its way back to the Imperial Fleet, it would have no doubt reported Bauang as an ideal place for an amphibious assault. That way, the enemy could outflank the defenders at San Juan. Blackburn therefore decided to send Charlie Youngblood further up the coast with a rifle platoon to establish an early-warning outpost. Since they had no radios, Blackburn instructed him to either send a runner or fire three shots if they detected any Japanese movement. Meanwhile, Blackburn and Newman would organize the rest of the company into a defensive line along the beach. Acknowledging his orders, Youngblood departed with his rifle platoon. It was the last time Don Blackburn would ever see him.

The Ilocanos finished digging their foxholes on the beach a few hours after sunset. As night descended over what remained of Headquarters Battalion, the wind settled down and the surf drew itself into a quiet whisper, slowly lulling Blackburn to sleep. Exhausted and emotionally fraught after the week's activity, he dozed off at his post in the sand. But after what seemed like only a few minutes, a hand emerged from the darkness and violently shook him by the shoulder.

"Don, wake up!" It was Shelby Newman.

"What is it?" Blackburn answered, rubbing the sleep from his eyes.

Newman reported seeing lights a few hundred yards off the beach. Blackburn's eyes flew open at the sound of the news and, jumping up from his foxhole, he discovered that Newman was correct. Lights. Hundreds of them, red and green. They were running lights that belonged to a faceless armada lingering somewhere off the coast.

"Any word from Charlie Youngblood?"

"No." Charlie hadn't fired off his shots or sent a runner. "What'll we do?"

"Wait." Blackburn replied. "That's all we can do."

Hours passed, and there was still no sign from Youngblood's platoon. Was he asleep? Blackburn didn't want to open up unless he knew the running lights were Japanese.

Finally, as the sun crept over the horizon, daylight revealed a sinister fleet of Japanese warships. Newman and Blackburn stood there agape. "The Jap transports and landing craft were out there en masse," Blackburn said. "We watched them getting in the boats, but we didn't have anything to shoot at them." The Ilocanos, beholding the same sight as Blackburn, shuddered in their foxholes and clung nervously to their rusty old Enfields. As the enemy landing craft barreled through the morning surf, Blackburn knew that there was only one order left to give.

"FIRE!"

All at once, the Enfields and machine guns opened up on the incoming vessels. Blackburn said that his Ilocanos, "were firing, and they were registering right on the landing craft. They were doing great. I thought, man, these guys are really tigers, but all of a sudden, *psst*, and it stopped." Blackburn went down to the machine gun nests to figure out what had happened. Apparently, the Filipinos had put their ammunition belts in the sand. Thus, when it came time to feed their rounds into the gun, the bolts jammed. "Well, with this, and those Japs coming across the beach," Blackburn added, "the Filipinos started taking off." The terrified Ilocanos fled from the beach in panic, dropping their rifles, canteens, and any equipment that might slow them down.

Blackburn and Newman tried to rally the fleeing troops. "Pick up your guns and fight, you bastards!" As the wave of Ilocanos flew past him, Don succeed in grabbing one soldier by the arm, spinning him around, and shoving a rifle into hands. It was no use. The terrified man dropped the rifle and continued running. As the Ilocanos disappeared into the coconut palms, Blackburn turned to see the wasteland they had left behind. Discarded Enfields, machine guns, and half-fed ammunition belts littered the beach. It was a pathetic sight. By now, the enemy landing craft had struck the mire and Blackburn could see the Nipponese warriors peeking over the sides of the vessels, cold grimaces and scowls on their faces.

Blackburn turned to Newman and shouted, "Let's get the hell out of here!"

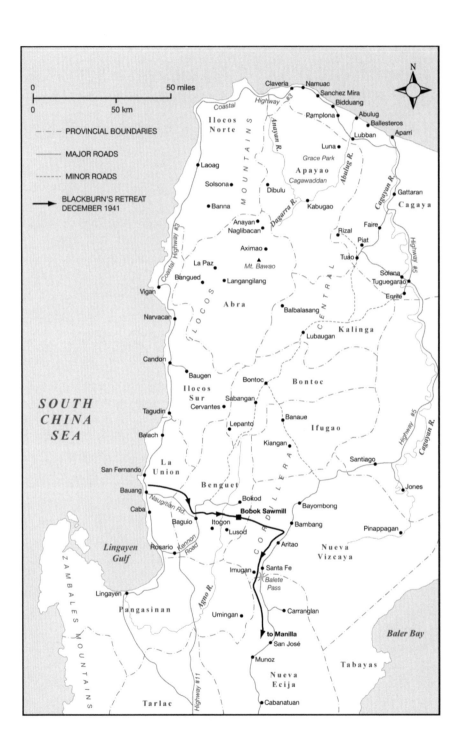

CHAPTER 3

THE ROAD TO BATAAN

T en miles inland from the shore at Bauang, Blackburn and Newman
caught up to the rest of the Allied retreat on the Nagulian Road.
Along the way, Blackburn recovered only a handful of the Ilocanos who
had fled from the beach; the others had disappeared into the wilderness,
never to be seen or heard from again. Farther down the road, amid the
sea of bodies in their frantic retreat, Blackburn and Newman found
other remnants of the 12th Infantry who had gone to reinforce Noble's
men at San Fernando. As it turned out, their Outpost Line of Resistance
had collapsed.

Under the heat of the morning sun, the retreating soldiers hobbled
down the Nagulian Road. Some could barely keep themselves upright.
Others hung their heads in a zombie-like trance with their rifles and
machine guns spread across their shoulders. Several more had piled into
the backseats of whatever vehicle had been nearby: troop carrier, Jeep,
Plymouth, or Chevrolet. It was a dismal horde of military trucks and
commandeered vehicles. And Don Blackburn recalled that "there
wasn't anything to think about except that we were in a hell of a mess."

Joined in the retreat by the 71st Infantry under Lieutenant Colonel
James Bonnett, Blackburn's regiment reached Nagulian proper shortly
before nine o' clock that morning. Once there, Don discovered everyone
awaiting the arrival of Colonel John P. Horan. Horan, commanding
officer of the 43rd Infantry Regiment (Philippine Scouts), now had the
unenviable task of stemming the tide of confusion in North Luzon.

Hoping to bring some semblance of order to the chaotic retreat, Horan called a meeting of all nearby officers to the marketplace in Nagulian. By order of the Division Commander, General Brougher, Horan announced that the 71st Infantry was to continue its withdrawal via the Kennon Road to the city of Rosario.

"What about the 12th Infantry?" Blackburn asked.

"I don't know," Horan said. He hadn't received any orders to that effect.

Sheepishly, one of Horan's staff officers suggested that the 12th and 13th Infantry simply follow the 71st down to Rosario. Horan dissented, however, saying that he would have to go back to Baguio and clear it with General Brougher.

But while Horan jumped into his command car and sped away to Baguio, Nagulian continued to swell with retreating soldiers. After a few hours, Lieutenant Colonel Bonnett decided he could take it no longer. With or without Horan's consent, Bonnett had to get the column moving again. He wasn't about to let Nagulian become a bottleneck, especially with a Japanese beachhead only fifteen miles away.

Thus the column once again plowed forward. Jumping into the back of a nearby Plymouth, Blackburn turned his head to see an old passenger bus speeding by. Its occupants were also members of the retreating column and its frontseat passengers were none other than Moses and Noble—both men wearing the unmistakable grimace of battle fatigue.

Later in the day, a few miles outside Baguio, Bonnett ordered the column to halt and directed every vehicle to pull off to either side of the road. Taking Moses and Noble with him, Bonnett left the column with orders to "wait here" while he went into Baguio to get some answers from Horan. Meanwhile, Blackburn and his comrades halted the Plymouth and looked behind them to see the Nagulian Road stretching down the mountainside, winding through the landscape to the China Sea, where the menacing warships of the Imperial Japanese Navy still loomed in the distance.

As the sun disappeared over the mountain, the column continued to wait. By now, most of the drivers had shut off their engines, and many of the soldiers had fallen asleep. But as midnight approached, there was still no sign of Bonnett. Blackburn wondered, "What could be taking him so long?"

Finally, Don and a few others decided to go into Baguio and find out for themselves. Firing up the old Plymouth, Don Blackburn directed the column up the mountainside and onto the plateau where Baguio stood. Settling the column into the City Park, Blackburn and Newman drove the Plymouth into Camp John Hay.

Inside the main conference room of the camp's headquarters, Blackburn found Colonel Horan along with Moses, Noble, and a slew of other senior officers. All of them clung nervously to their cigarettes, filling the room with a smoky haze so thick that Don could barely see five feet in front of him. Horan stood at the head of the table.

The problem, according to Horan, was the Kennon Road. The Kennon Road led to Highway 1, the only thoroughfare with access to Rosario and the Central Plains. To get the column moving again, they would have to use the Kennon Road to join the other retreating regiments in Central Luzon. The only problem was that this road was supposedly blocked by the Japanese.

"Why don't we get a machine gun, mount it on a Jeep, and go down the Kennon Road?" one officer suggested. A machine gun team could make a hasty reconnaissance and be back within two hours. Sadly, nothing came of his suggestion.

"God damn it, we ought to defend Baguio!" another officer bellowed.

After all, they had enough of everything to draw the Japanese into an urban battle: guns, ammunition, and a maze of tunnels underneath the city. Blackburn also remembered that "Baguio was the center of a big mining district. Most of the mines, as the story went, had about six months to a year's supply of food and quantities of weapons, and a lot of the miners were Reservists." Horan considered it for a moment, but opted not to destroy "this beautiful city."

Another officer chimed in, "Why don't we radio MacArthur and ask him?"

"We can't," Horan replied. "I had the code books burned this morning."

This war conference was quickly devolving into a comedy of errors. "I, as a First Lieutenant," Blackburn said, "was bug-eyed hearing all this foolishness." Finally, someone suggested an escape route through Highway 5. If the Kennon Road was blocked to the west, the column could travel east to a town called Bobok, and follow one of its horse trails down the east side of the mountain to Highway 5. But could the horse trail be made to accommodate vehicular traffic? No one knew for certain, but someone suggested that the manager of the Bobok Sawmill, an American named Ken Jorgensen, could tell them.

A call was put through to the Bobok Sawmill and, when asked if the horse trail could be expanded to accommodate a military convoy, Jorgensen simply answered "yes." Thus, the 2,000-man column uprooted itself from the Baguio City Park and headed towards Bobok. Upon their arrival, an anxious Lieutenant Colonel Bonnett cornered Ken Jorgensen and asked him how long it would take to make the horse trail accessible for a convoy.

His reply: "Anywhere from three to six months."

The officers gasped in disbelief. How could this critical detail have been overlooked? Jorgensen innocently replied that he had been asked only if the trail could be made passable, not how long it would take. Bonnett suddenly realized that he had led his column into a virtual dead end. They couldn't return to Baguio and their only escape route was a horse trail which had to be taken by foot.

Regaining his composure, Bonnett ordered the column to abandon its vehicles and launch them over the side of the mountain, lest the Japanese try to salvage anything for their own use. So Blackburn, Newman, and the other officers took turns driving their vehicles off the side of a cliff, jumping to safety just before the old cars plummeted into the valley below.

The following morning, Christmas Day 1941, the ragtag column proceeded on foot, down the rocky horse trail to Highway 5. After two days on the trail, the column staggered into a small barrio called Pingkian, where Blackburn finally had the opportunity to rest his swollen, blistered feet. Enjoying a small meal of rice and bananas with a local family, Blackburn hobbled over to Major Moses.

"Where do we go from here, sir?"

Moses said that he and Noble were staying behind to keep the trailing elements of the column moving along. Meanwhile, Bonnett and most of his men were headed to Aritao, another barrio just a few miles south. Don decided to go into Aritao as well, but the news that awaited him there was hardly encouraging. Upon Blackburn's arrival, Bonnett announced that he had just gotten off the phone with Major Enriques, one of Horan's staff officers. According to the conversation, the units defending Balete Pass had withdrawn, and the Japanese now had a foothold in San Jose. Essentially, Bonnett explained, the 12th, 13th, and 71st Infantry were now cut off. They had no reliable transportation or communication beyond Nueva Vizcaya province. Now, Bonnett said, there was only one thing left to do: dissolve the column and return control of the units to their respective commanders. The 12th and 13th Infantry were on their own.

Bonnett planned to take his men farther east into the "unexplored territory" inhabited by the Ilongots, savages colloquially known as the "Longhairs." Blackburn didn't know what Bonnett expected to accomplish by this move, but he nonetheless phoned the news to Major Moses in Pingkian. Blackburn also told Moses that he and Shelby Newman were organizing their own expedition to Manila. It was a risky move, Blackburn explained, but he refused to resign himself to the hopelessness preached by Bonnett.

"You make your own personal decision," Moses replied, "but have the men of the 12th Infantry—what's left of them—put on their civilian clothes and go to their homes." With that, Don Blackburn let out an enormous sigh of relief. No longer did he have to worry about his slovenly, undisciplined Ilocanos. And the disinterested soldiers were more than happy to shed their uniforms.

Finally free from his apathetic charges, Blackburn and Newman commandeered a Philippine Army truck for their ride to Manila. Joining them were two other officers, Eddie Bliss and George Williams. Together, the foursome busted out the windshield and punched holes in the tailgate, placing automatic rifles at either end. They soon realized that fortune had smiled on them that day; for in the midst of creating their "armored truck," they found several sticks of dynamite piled in the truck bed. Blackburn marveled at the sight; he and his comrades now had makeshift hand grenades.

At about three o'clock that afternoon, December 26, the "armored truck" rumbled into Bambang. Since the invasion, Bambang had become headquarters of the North Luzon Force, temporarily set up in the plantation home of a wealthy cane farmer. Pulling up to the porch of the elegant stone house, Blackburn could see General Jonathan M. Wainwright, commander of the North Luzon Force, seated on the porch with his entourage. As Don Blackburn dismounted the armored truck,

Wainwright sat with a cool yet stern look upon his face—as if he were determined to get the story of what had happened up north from these young, disheveled officers. Approaching the General, Blackburn couldn't help but notice the contrast between Wainwright's appearance and his own. The General looked clean, crisp, and meticulously well groomed. Blackburn, with his uniform tattered and caked with dirt, felt a tingling apprehension as he slumped into the chair across the porch from his Commanding General.

The General wasted no time in getting to the point. "What the hell is going on up there?" Blackburn recounted the story of what had happened from Bauang to Baguio; from Baguio to Bobok; and from Bobok to Artiao. Wainwright shook his head in disbelief, but the stern look slowly disappeared from his face. After detecting the change in the General's mood, Blackburn requested permission to continue his travels to Manila. Wainwright granted his request, but only on the condition that Blackburn gave a full account of his story to USAFFE Headquarters once he arrived. Acknowledging the order, Blackburn saluted and turned to leave. But as he made his way to the armored truck, Newman and Williams stopped him. They had changed their minds about the trip to Manila and decided that they were in good enough shape to rejoin the 11th Division from here. The 12th Infantry Regiment may have been no more, but Newman and Williams were certain that Division could find something for them to do. Taken aback by their sudden change of heart, Blackburn wished them luck and continued the rest of his journey with Eddie Bliss in tow.

Back on Highway 5, Bliss and Blackburn arrived in Manila a few hours after sundown. Despite the Japanese bombardment, both men were surprised to see that the city had retained much of its antebellum splendor. But even more surprising to Blackburn were the attitudes of the local citizenry; some of them carried on as if it were "business as usual." Even the Manila-Corregidor ferry was still operating—an opportunity that Eddie Bliss took to return to his original unit, a coastal artillery battery on Corregidor.

Parting ways with Bliss, Blackburn drove to the Army-Navy Club where, for the first time in weeks, he was treated to a bed, bath, and fresh uniforms. Spending the night in the peaceful confines of the Army-Navy Club, Blackburn awoke the next morning and hired a horse-drawn cab to take him to the USAFFE Headquarters. Just as he had promised General Wainwright, he gave a full account of his story to General Richard Marshall, MacArthur's Deputy Chief of Staff.

Blackburn decided that his last order of business before rejoining the 11th Division would be to place a call at the Manila Telephone Exchange. His timing was impeccable as the Army Signal Corps had taken over the building and were planning to blow it up at nine o' clock that evening. It was barely 12:45 in the afternoon when Blackburn asked the officer-in-charge, a young Captain, how long it would take to connect a call to Columbus, Georgia—Don wanted to hear Ann's voice just one more time. The Captain replied that it would take about eight hours.

This didn't sit well with Blackburn; for even if the call did take eight hours to complete, it wouldn't allow him any buffer time before they blew up the Exchange. Luckily, at eight-fifteen that night, Don was notified by the hotel staff at the Army-Navy Club that his call had gone through. Rushing to the front desk, Don scrambled for the phone before he was stopped by the concierge—guests were not allowed to make long distance calls unless they had a Club membership.

That did it. Blackburn finally lost his temper.

He snarled at the concierge that he was going to make the call whether anyone liked it or not. Seeing the Colt .45 dangling from Blackburn's hip, the concierge wisely backed down. "While talking on the phone," Blackburn said, "every time I'd say something, the censor would get on the line, so it wasn't a very satisfactory conservation. The only thing I said to her was, 'You know, things are a little tight out here right now, but just don't worry. I'm going to make it.' That's about all you could repeat, otherwise you'd be cut off." Don never gave any further details about the call he placed to Ann that night, other than to say that he loved her. His was the last phone call made from Manila that night.

The following morning, as Blackburn prepared to leave the Army-Navy Club, his departure was interrupted by the arrival of Major John Primrose, a staff officer from the 11th Division. He had apparently come to Army-Navy to pick up reinforcements for the continuing fight in Central Luzon. Don mentioned that he had been with the 12th Infantry, and Primrose filled him in on what had happened since the column's dissolution at Aritao. The Division Headquarters, Primrose said, had relocated to the town of Mexico in Pampanga province. And even though the 12th and 13th Infantry had lost several men, a few companies from both regiments had also made it to Pampanga.

Rather than make the trip to Division Headquarters alone, Blackburn decided to hand over his armored truck to USAFFE authorities and hitch a ride with Major Primrose into Pampanga. At Mexico, forty-five miles northwest of Manila, Blackburn reported to General Brougher. Recalling that this young Lieutenant had experience with military communications, Brougher promptly made him the new Division Signals Officer. The previous Signals Officer, Brougher explained, had unfortunately "taken a wrong road and had been picked up or killed by the Japs."

Now a member of Division Staff, Blackburn felt more like a beleaguered bureaucrat than a soldier. It vaguely reminded him of the time he had spent as an instructor during his days with the 12th Infantry—substandard equipment, improvising with minimal results, and making recommendations that ultimately fell on deaf ears.

On January 2, 1942, Blackburn was once again reunited with Harry Kuykendall, the perennial pessimist he had met at Fort Benning. Kuykendall had had a particularly rough time since the invasion. His unit with the Philippine Scouts had been in continuous combat with the Japanese since mid-December. Blackburn met up with Kuykendall as the 11th Division was readjusting its front line near the town of Guagua. Just as before, Kuykendall was up to his fatalistic fortune-telling: "My number is just about up. They'll get me within the next 48 hours." It was the last of Kuykendall's doomsday prophecies to come true. The following day, he was killed in action.

Despite the overall insipidity of being Division Signals Officer, Blackburn was never at a loss for words in his diary.

> January 4: Most of 11th Division concentrated at Hermosa. Japs spot us and bomb and strafe the hell out of the Division. Many killed and wounded and the town left a burning mass. Division ordered into rest area west of Balanga, Bataan.

In the opening days of 1942, the 11th Division consolidated itself within the confines of the Bataan Peninsula. Under the execution of "War Plan Orange," USAFFE's final defense of Luzon was to take place on

Bataan and Corregidor. Blackburn knew—as did many others—that this was their last chance to stave off the Japanese. He had heard in passing that reinforcements were on their way from the US—but would there be anything left to reinforce by the time they arrived? He tried not to think about it.

> Jaunary 11: Division ordered on Beach defense along Manila Bay from Abucay to Limay. Bataan Reports received, to effect that Japs have received heavy casualties in attempts to break through our M.L.R [Main Line of Resistance] Abucay-Moran Defense line. Our artillery has been doing a superb job.
> January 12–26: Jap planes seen and heard continuously, with none of ours in sight. They bomb and strafe anything and everything they see. Received my promotion to Captain on January 21, 1942. Japs came through on the left of the Philippine Division in 51st Division Sector, it is reported.

On January 30, the Japanese began to tighten their noose around Bataan. Blackburn recalled that they penetrated the Main Line of Resistance near the Toul River, creating two enemy pockets that stood for nearly a month.

> January 31: Japs discovered behind our M.L.R. only 200 yards from 11th Infantry Command Post. 11th Infantry [Division] has a front of about 2,000 yards which is considerable when you consider the density of the jungle and what's left of our Division. The route used by the Japs was the Toul River, which is just a stream in the dry season.
> February 15 and thereabouts: The Japs hit and penetrated the 11th Infantry M.L.R.—checked after forming a second pocket. The original pocket known as the Toul Pocket still exists.
> February 20 or 21: The two pockets finally cleaned out after tough fighting [Blackburn didn't know it, but there were actually three pockets].

Around this time, Don became well acquainted with Major Russell Volckmann. Volckmann had commanded the 11th Infantry Regiment

during its retreat to Bataan and now joined the Division Staff as its chief
Intelligence Officer. Billeted in the same nipa palm hut, he and Blackburn often traded stories about their time in combat. In public, Volckmann and Blackburn respected their differences in rank. In private,
however, they quickly became best friends.

March was relatively quiet on the USAFFE front. But by the first
week of April, the situation on Bataan had become hopeless. Nearly
half of the men had succumbed to malaria and several others had begun
feeding off of whatever plants or animals they could find. The worst
news, however, came on April 9: the commander of the Philippine II
Corps, General Edward P. King, had surrendered. This meant that the
entire western flank of the USAFFE defenses had collapsed and the
Japanese would be at the 11th Division command post in a matter of
hours.

That evening, General Brougher ordered the first of the white flags
to be raised over the Division compound. Meanwhile, Blackburn and
Volckmann were beside themselves in disbelief. *Surrender?* They didn't
quite like it. Both men knew the Japanese were going to win this fight,
but they saw no reason to surrender to their brand of savagery. After
all, if their occupation of Manchuria was any indication of how Japanese soldiers conducted themselves, an occupation of the Philippines
would certainly be no different.

Discussing their options, Russ Volckmann recalled some intelligence
reports he had collected from Division headquarters. The latest reports
confirmed that a few Philippine Army regiments had been caught
behind the lines in the Mountain Province of North Luzon. As the front
lines moved farther south, some of these regiments continued to harass
the Japanese's rear echelons while others had simply dissolved into the
wilderness. The game was over on Bataan, but Volckmann and Blackburn knew that if they could escape to the north, they might have a
chance to carry on a resistance movement against the Japanese. Blackburn later recalled:

> The sparsely inhabited Cordilleras were sandwiched between
> the narrow Illocos coastal lowlands bordering the China Sea
> on the west and the Cagayan Valley on the east. To the south
> lay the Central Plain. Five principal Igorot tribes inhabited the
> area—the Benguets, Ifugaos, Bontocs, Kalingas, and Apayaos,

whose respectively named sub-provinces comprised the larger Mountain Province. The Igorots of this relatively inaccessible and invigorating region had benefited from early American administrators and missionaries, and gratitude was evidenced in their kindly attitude toward Americans. We knew the territory and approached it with confidence in the security and support that it would provide.

Deep down, Volckmann and Blackburn knew that their chances of reaching Mountain Province were slim to none. Roaming bandits, Japanese patrols, and the endless network of enemy spies would make their journey into North Luzon a difficult one. But all things considered, both men knew it was better to take their chances in the jungle than to rely on the "hospitality" of a Japanese prison camp.

Later that evening, while Blackburn gathered some supplies for their journey (including a wool blanket, quinine, and emergency rations), Volckmann told General Brougher of their intentions to escape. Brougher unenthusiastically told Volckmann that he could do so if they wished, adding sheepishly that "If I were a younger man, I would entertain such thoughts myself."

But barely a few moments after Volckmann departed General Brougher's hut, the Japanese burst through the perimeter of the Division compound. Startled by the sudden blaze of gunfire, Volckmann turned to see the enemy muzzle flashes penetrating from the darkness. Ducking to the ground in terror, he scrambled back to the hut he shared with Blackburn.

"Don, let's get the hell out of here!"

With the fiery onslaught of the Rising Sun now only moments behind them, Volckmann and Blackburn jumped over a nearby embankment, hurdling themselves into the darkness of the jungle.

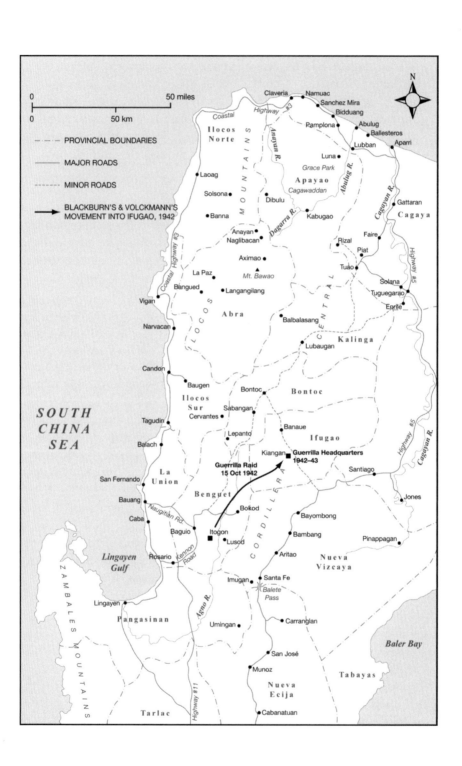

0
50 miles

0
50 km

- - - · PROVINCIAL BOUNDARIES

——— MAJOR ROADS

- - - - - MINOR ROADS

➤ BLACKBURN'S & VOLCKMANN'S
MOVEMENT INTO IFUGAO, 1942

Claveria   Namuac

Sanchez Mira

Bidduang

Coastal   *Highway #3*   Pamplona   Abulug   Ballesteros

Ilocos   Lubban   Aparri
Norte

Luna

Grace Park

Laoag   **Apayao**

Solsona   Dibulu   *Cagawaddan*   Rizal   Faire

Banna   Kabugao   Piat   **Cagaya**

Anayan   Tuao   Gattaran
Naglibacan

Aximao   Solana
                                ▲   Tuguegarao
                            Mt. Bawao

La Paz   Enrile

Bangued   Langangilang

Vigan   **Abra**   Balbalasang

Narvacan   **Kalinga**

                                        Lubaugan

Candon

Baugen   Bontoc   **Bontoc**

Ilocos
Sur   Sabangan

Tagudin   Cervantes   Banaue   **Ifugao**

                Lepanto

SOUTH   Kiangan   **Guerrilla Headquarters**
CHINA   **1942–43**
SEA   Balach   Santiago

                        Guerrilla Raid
                        15 Oct 1942

San Fernando   **La**   Jones
                Union

Bauang   *Naugitian Rd.*   **Benguet**   Bokod   Bayombong

Caba   Bambang   Pinappagan

Baguio   Itogon
                Lusod   Aritao   **Nueva**
Lingayen   Rosario   *Kennon*   **Vizcaya**
Gulf   *Road*

                Imugan   Santa Fe
Lingayen   *Balete*
                                Pass
Pangasinan
                Umingan   Carranglan   *Baler Bay*

                        San José   **Tabayas**

                Munoz

                Nueva
                Ecija

Tarlac   Cabanatuan

CHAPTER 4

PERILOUS JOURNEY

Don Blackburn tumbled head over feet into the nearby creek bed—hitting the gravelly bottom with a raspy thump as he landed next to Volckmann. Dropping to their bellies, the two men shimmied their way out of the pre-dawn massacre. Behind him, Blackburn could hear the screams of his dying comrades, punctuated by the shrill melody of Japanese gunfire.

Neither man knew how long they crawled through the creek bed that night, but after what seemed like hours, both were exhausted and badly scraped from the night's maneuvers. "Let's wait until dawn to see if the Japs are moving through," Blackburn said. As he and Volckmann agreed on a stopping point for the night, the pair settled themselves onto a nearby embankment and quickly fell asleep. A few hours later, however, they were startled awake by the sound of voices.

Volckmann motioned for Blackburn to keep quiet as they jumped to their feet. The mysterious voices were coming from the other side of the creek bed. Out from the shadows, Blackburn emerged to find that these voices belonged to four Philippine Army soldiers and an American lieutenant named Whiteman. Whiteman asked to join Blackburn and Volckmann in their travels northward, to which the four Filipinos added that they could serve as guides and interpreters. Volckmann initially resisted the Filipinos' offer (he had wanted to keep his traveling party small), but seeing how adamant they were to fight the Japanese, he let them into the group.

As daylight crept through the crevices of the jungle canopy, Blackburn realized that their maneuvers from the previous night had put them only one mile from the Division command post. Undaunted, however, the seven of them continued northward, leaving the creek bed and descending into the darkest depths of the Bataan jungle. Although dawn had come, it was of little use—the foliage so thick that none of them could see more than fifteen feet in any direction. Every step was greeted by a crackle of twigs underfoot, followed by a slosh of muddy soil under the other foot. While pushing aside the clutter of leaves and branches, Don Blackburn's movement was further hindered by the rattan vines that constantly smacked him in the face.

After they had gone about three miles, Blackburn and Volckmann recognized the area as a former sector of the 1st Division. They decided to rest for a while and Blackburn, reaching into the musette bag he had packed before the surrender, felt nothing but an empty hole. Disgusted, he realized that the rattan vines had ripped open his bag, and most of its contents had been lost to the jungle. Blackburn had packed as many C-rations as the bag could carry, but now all that remained were some biscuits, two cans of meat, and a small packet of dehydrated coffee. Don crumbled the biscuits, mixing them in some water from a nearby stream, and distributed the concoction amongst the seven men in the group. However, these were the only rations they had—and Don knew it wouldn't last long among the seven of them.

Wondering where he could find more food, he soon realized that his options were virtually non-existent. There were no towns or marketplaces in the immediate area, and the closest farm, Abucay Hacienda, was still occupied by the Japanese.

Volckmann, meanwhile, reached into his own bag and pulled out his map of Bataan. Consulting with Blackburn, they decided to lead the group northward to Trail 5, the closest man-made trail to their current position. As they walked on, Blackburn could hear the sound of artillery shells landing in the distance. Once, it had sounded good to him, "but that was when American artillery had been in action."

A few hours before sunset, the group came upon Trail 5. Not wanting to continue their abusive hike through the jungle, Blackburn and the others proceeded down the trail at a cautious pace. After a few moments on the trail, however, the group came upon a Japanese soldier leaning against a nearby tree. Terrified, the seven of them dove for cover into the underbrush. From underneath the cover of different shrubs, Blackburn and Volckmann peered at the enemy soldier. After several minutes, both men noticed that the soldier wasn't moving. Volckmann slowly inched his way closer to the unmoving enemy before finally realizing that the soldier was dead. Apparently, someone had propped him up against the tree. Shaking off their fright from the dead sentry, the seven men quickly sprang from their hiding places and continued down the trail.

The journey along Trail 5 continued without incident, and at sundown they reached the former sector of the 12th Infantry, where the regiment "had fought one of its last losing battles" on Bataan. The group settled down for the night, but Don Blackburn's imagination began to run away with him. Perhaps still shaken from his encounter with the dead soldier, he found it impossible to sleep. Several times throughout the night, he woke up Volckmann saying that he heard enemy sounds from beyond the trail. During the retreat, both men learned that the Japanese used a system of bird calls and cricket chirps to communicate at night. Volckmann convinced Blackburn that it was just his imagination, but moments later Blackburn woke him up again. Now he reported seeing enemy flashlights. Little did Blackburn know that these "flashlights" were nothing more than the shifting foliage allowing the moon and starlight to shine through. Volckmann once again tried to convince Blackburn that his mind was playing tricks on him, but the young Captain would have none of it—he couldn't sleep unless they moved to another hiding spot. With a sigh of reluctance, Volckmann relocated the group a mere fifty yards, but it was enough to calm Blackburn's nerves and finally put him to sleep.

The next morning, the group returned to Trail 5 where they reached the Pilar-Bagac Road by noon. Pilar-Bagac had once been USAFFE's Main Line of Resistance, but now the signs of defeat lay scattered everywhere—shell casings, empty magazines, and a demolished tank whose fire had not yet burned out. They crossed Pilar-Bagac at Kilometer Post 144, where Don Blackburn noticed a small schoolhouse standing prominently on the other side of the road. Blackburn remembered that it had been an artillery target during the defense of Bataan. The 11th Division "had fired at it constantly because it had been reported as an enemy command post." But whatever the schoolhouse had been, "it had come through the shelling unscathed."

Shifting their direction to the northeast, Blackburn and his comrades began climbing the southern slope of Mt. Natib. For now, they had left the protective canopy of the jungle and the midday sun beat down on them mercilessly. Soaked with perspiration, and running out of rations, Blackburn's mind once again returned to the topic of food. Fortunately, on "the second day out, we all of a sudden hit a ravine. We looked down and gazed upon a Jap bivouac area," Blackburn said. The site had been abandoned but the Japanese had left behind several bits of food. "I went down and scrounged around and, sure enough, I found some onions and a little bit of Jap food."

The following morning, they came upon another Japanese bivouac. From atop a nearby hill, Volckmann sent Blackburn down to investigate. Don meandered his way down into the bivouac and, sensing that it was unoccupied, casually foraged for any leftover rations. He didn't find any food, but noticed that the Japanese had made a faucet from a bamboo tube which they had pushed into a nearby stream. While filling his canteen, he looked back up to find Volckmann in a state of panic—"jumping up and down like the man out of a jack-in-the-box, waving his hands, and motioning me to get out of there." Blackburn didn't need it give it a second thought; he hastily re-capped the lid of his canteen and scrambled back up the hill to Volckmann and the others. "When I got back to him and looked, right around the corner from where I had been, some Japs were sitting." Blackburn and his posse hastily fled from the bivouac. "We didn't hang around long enough to count them, or to figure out what they were doing."

For the next few days, scavenging enemy bivouacs became a regular affair. On the fourth day of their travels, they stumbled onto a trail that led to a house about a mile downhill. From their current position, none of them could tell if the house was occupied, but two of the Filipino soldiers volunteered to search it for any food or water. Blackburn and the others waited, but the two Filipinos never returned from their errand. Apparently, they had decided that travelling with the Americans was no longer in their best interest.

The following morning, April 14, Blackburn came upon a road in the vicinity of Abucay Hacienda. Not wanting to force his way through the jungle again, he and Volckmann decided to try their luck along the road. Their luck, however, quickly ran out, as a Japanese cavalry unit came thundering around the bend. "We couldn't do anything but just hope that they didn't see us," and the five of them dashed into a nearby sugarcane field. Blackburn, Volckmann, and Whiteman re-grouped on the other side of the cane field, but the two remaining Filipinos were never seen again. Like their comrades the day before, they too had apparently grown weary of travelling with these Americans. From then on, Blackburn and Volckmann decided to stay off the road.

Exhausted from their latest close encounter, Don and the others settled down for a late afternoon's rest. The three of them were collectively in their worst shape since the start of the invasion. On the day he assumed command of Headquarters Battalion, Don had been a healthy 180 pounds. Now, his weight hovered just above 125. Unlike many of his comrades, Blackburn had not yet succumbed to the ravages of malaria, dysentery or yellow fever, but he was unsure how much longer his health would last.

The following morning, the group made their way around Abucay Hacienda before picking up another northbound trail. Here, they encountered another Filipino who identified himself as a retired Philippine Scout. He invited Blackburn and the group into what he called an "evacuation camp." According to the old scout, these camps had sprung up all over Luzon. In the wake of the Japanese onslaught, civilians who had lost their homes and their livelihoods fled to the wilderness, intent on waiting out the occupation.

At the sergeant's camp, Blackburn was treated to a hot meal of beef and rice—the first full meal he had enjoyed since the fall of Bataan. He was also surprised to see that, among the sergeant's guests, were two other American officers: a pair of Army Air Corps lieutenants named Petit and Anderson. As Blackburn and Volckmann sat down to chat with their newfound Air Corps friends, they learned the fates of Moses and Noble. During their final days in Bataan, the pair had been promoted to Lieutenant Colonel and had escaped along with a handful of other Americans. According to Petit and Anderson, the Colonels were last seen headed north to a camp in the Zambales Mountains purportedly run by Major Claude Thorp. It was good news, and Blackburn was delighted hear that Moses and Noble had survived the debacle in Bataan.

The following morning, Blackburn, Volckmann, Whiteman, and the two Air Corps lieutenants hit the trail northbound to Highway 7. After only a few paces, they encountered yet another Filipino. Out of the wilderness emerged a young man of no more than nineteen years old. Dressed in a tattered Philippine Army uniform, this young man spoke English fluently and identified himself as "Bruno." "Our Boy Bruno," as the group would call him, was a Philippine Army Corporal and a member of the Igorot tribe. Don knew that the Igorot tribesmen came from good stock: they were hearty, resilient, disciplined, and enjoyed a much better reputation within the Philippine Army than did the Illocanos.

Back on the trail, the posse arrived at Banban around midday. Banban was a small barrio situated just one mile south of Highway 7, the northern boundary of the Bataan Peninsula. Here, Don felt as though his luck had finally started to change: he had survived his initial forays into the jungle, escaped from the jaws of the Japanese, and had found Filipinos who were sympathetic to the American cause. "When we got to the northern fringes of Bataan . . . the Death March had started and the people were horrified at what they observed, and terrified of the Japs. They just despised them. So as a result, there was a fair chance that you could talk to any of them and they would protect you. It varied; some of them were nervous as cats if you were with them, because they knew if the Japs ever caught you with them, they were going to be killed. So you just had to read the tea leaves and see if you wanted to push on or not."

Luckily, the "tea leaves" at Banban spelled good tidings for Don Blackburn. The barrio chieftain invited his American guests to partake in a feast honoring the return of a local son. Chicken, beef, rice, and copious gallons of wine made their way around the table as Blackburn stuffed himself with the native fare. After the day's festivities, the jovial chieftain agreed to take the Americans beyond Highway 7. Once, the highway had been the 11th Infantry's Main Line of Resistance—now it was a heavily patrolled enemy thoroughfare leading to the Japanese naval base at Olongapo. The group prepared to leave Banban a few hours after sundown, but Whiteman—now in the midst of a crippling fever—elected to stay behind. The villagers agreed to look after him and the stalwart lieutenant said that he would continue north as soon as his fever broke. Blackburn wished him well and departed Banban with Volckmann, Bruno, Petit, and Anderson. Sadly, they would never see Whiteman again. His fever continued to worsen and he passed away at Banban two weeks later.

On April 18, 1942, Blackburn crossed Highway 7 without incident. Until now, he had been untouched by tropical disease, but scarcely an hour after crossing the highway, he and Volckmann became violently sick. "Dysentery and malaria hit us."

Sensing the change in his guests' health, their guide from Banban diverted the group into a nearby evacuation camp run by a man named Guerrero. Guerrero had several friends in Banban and, like many other Filipinos, he had fled to the jungle after the Japanese destroyed his home. "The Guerrero family lived right outside of Dinalupihan . . . they had an evacuation hut, and they put us out in another little grass hut near theirs. They'd bring food to us and take care of us the best they could."

As the Banban guide left the two sickly Americans in Guerrero's care, Blackburn staggered into the hut and collapsed on its bamboo floor. Don could hardly believe it—within a matter of hours, the malaria had robbed him of all his normal faculties.

Blackburn was able to recall his stay at Guerrero's only through spurts of intermittent consciousness. He would be cognizant long enough to see the Guerreros' daughters, Mili and Mimi, bringing him a small bowl of rice, vegetables, or meat. Other times, he would awaken to the sound of Mili washing his filthy uniform outside the hut. More frequently, however, he would awaken to the sound of buzzing mosquitoes—or to the sharp pangs of his relentless dysentery.

Although he could barely maintain consciousness, Don never faltered in showing his appreciation to Guerrero. The old patriarch had taken an incredible risk in harboring these Americans. And Blackburn couldn't even imagine the fate that would befall Guerrero if the Japanese discovered his complicity. And yet, neither Guerrero, his wife, nor their daughters ever complained about giving refuge to Blackburn and Volckmann.

Despite the continuous care, however, Blackburn's health wasn't improving. Finally, on June 1, Guerrero secured him and Volckmann a doctor's visit outside Dinalupihan. Loading his frail guests onto the back of a small sled, Guerrero hauled them into the doctor's garage. Don couldn't remember much about the visit—and he wasn't even sure if the man he saw was a real doctor—but he nonetheless received some shots of quinine and was feeling better within a few hours.

Returning to the evacuation hut a few days later, Don found that

Petit and Anderson had left. According to Bruno, the two Air Corpsmen decided to continue their travels northward into the Zambales Mountains. Over the following week, Blackburn regained his normal strength and, by the middle of June, staying conscious was no longer a fleeting affair. In the middle of Blackburn's convalescence, Petit returned to Guerrero's camp to deliver some heartening news: while he and Anderson had been searching for other Americans, they had stumbled upon another evacuation camp run by two brothers named Bill and Martin Fassoth. The Fassoths were plantation owners and had set up their camp deep in within the Zambales Mountains. According to Petit, the Fassoths had taken in about sixty American soldiers, most of whom were fall-outs from the Bataan Death March. Their ranks included an Army doctor who had a small supply of medicine and ran a small infirmary out of the camp.

Blackburn, fascinated by the news, resolved to make Fassoth Camp his next stop. Then, too, he hated the thought of leaving Guerrero. Over the past two months, Guerrero had given Blackburn much and asked for very little. He had risked his life and his resources helping two Americans who were practically strangers. But Blackburn knew that he and Volckmann were, first and foremost, military officers, and they had a mission to accomplish. Reluctantly, he turned down Guerrero's invitation to stay. Don recounted the most emotional event of his travels as he bid goodbye to the Guerreros on June 22. He owed them a debt he knew he could never repay.

Grimly, Don Blackburn set his feet on the trail to the Zambales Highlands. His malaria had relapsed but this time he refused to let it slow down his travels. Three hours into the journey, however, Don began to regret his decision—the merciless heat plundered what little endurance he had left. Shortly before midnight, and only a few miles from the perimeter of Fassoth Camp, he collapsed.

Once again, through fleeting bouts of consciousness, Blackburn could sense himself being picked up and carried into a bamboo enclosure. When the malaria finally remitted, he awoke to find himself safely within the confines of Fassoth Camp.

Blackburn had never seen anything like it. The camp was even better than it had been described. He arose from his bunk bed to find himself inside a quaint little barracks made entirely from bamboo. The primitive barracks boasted ten beds on either side of the room—enough to hold forty men. Outside, the residents of the camp busied themselves tending to the needs of their mountain refuge. According to Don, "What happened here was that the Fassoths owned a large sugar plantation and right next door to the Fassoths . . . was another sugar plantation owned by a Spanish/Filipino mestizo named Vicente Bernia. They were neighbors and very good friends. When the death march was going on, American soldiers would fall out along the roadside and Filipinos would often pick them up before the Japs could detect them. But, they couldn't take care of them in their homes. They knew the Fassoths were American, so all of a sudden, they started taking these people to the Fassoths' hacienda. The Fassoths apparently got with Bernia and said, 'You know, we can't run an American hotel at this hacienda very long or it's going to be detected.' That's when they agreed that they would move and establish a camp in the mountains."

Vicente Bernia, meanwhile, was the chief financier behind the project. A wealthy man with great influence in the region, he corralled the locals into helping the displaced GIs, and procured medicine from the Catholic Archdiocese in Manila.

Blackburn's enthusiasm for the camp, however, quickly soured. On the morning after his and Volckmann's arrival, they were cornered by Sergeant Red Floyd, an American artilleryman. Gruff and physically imposing, Floyd had appointed himself the camp's de-facto strongman. "Now look, let's get the name of the game straight," he snarled. "If you guys want to stay here I want you to recognize that there is no such thing as rank. The war is over. If you want to play by our rules, fine. If you don't, you can get out of here."

Blackburn and Volckmann stared at each other in disbelief. How could Floyd have strongarmed the entire camp? Don was determined to get to the bottom of it.

As it turned out, Floyd's insubordination had begun in early May. During his initial tirade, Floyd said, "Those officers over there will sit and tell us to do this, and do that . . . and we are just as sick as they are." Fed up with their condescension and their refusal to work, Floyd and the others rebelled. Blackburn didn't approve of the insubordination, but by hearing Floyd out, he had taken the first step to restoring civility within the camp.

The next day, Red Floyd started complaining about the dysentery that had taken over the camp. Sensing an opportunity, Blackburn chimed in, "If some of the people around here had brains, something could be done about it."

"What do you mean?" Floyd bellowed.

"Well, you're running the camp and there isn't any such thing as a slit trench or a latrine around here. All you do with your business is throw it out of the window. All that great food that you cook in there is covered with flies that come off of that stuff, or don't you understand that?"

"Well," Floyd snapped, "who's going to dig us a trench?"

"Everybody will pitch in and dig. Now can you get your guys to pitch in? Are you willing to pitch in?" Blackburn asked.

"We got them all to work," Blackburn said. "Gradually, Red and his men started coming to us asking for advice in those areas where they felt inadequate . . . soon everyone was participating and not sitting on their duffs griping and passing out advice. As a result, things improved." Little by little, the officers at the camp regained their recognition as the men distanced themselves from Floyd and his resentful leadership.

While discussing their next move, Blackburn and Volckmann were joined by another Filipino, Sergeant Emilio Gumabay of the Philippine Constabulary. After the invasion, Emilio had been falsely accused of collaborating with the Americans. Now as a fugitive running from the Kempai-Tai, he had wandered into Fassoth Camp looking for anyone still interested in carrying on against the Japanese. Impressed by his tenacity, Volckmann invited the wayward police officer into their group.

Volckmann estimated that the four of them could reach North Luzon before New Year's if they left Fassoth Camp by September 1. Volckmann and Blackburn had heard from Bernia that two Lieutenant Colonels, Peter Cayler and Claude Thorp, were commanding small bands of guerrillas in Tarlac Province, only a few miles north. Volckmann knew Cayler personally; the two had met aboard the USS *Grant* en route to Philippines two years earlier. Taken prisoner at Bataan, Cayler had escaped from the Death March and had been taken in by a Chinese family named Jinco. Under the Jinco's care, Cayler had taken in four other Americans and had begun planning guerrilla operations against the Japanese. Claude Thorp, however, had a much different story. Prior to the invasion, he had been the Provost Marshal of the North Luzon Force. According to Blackburn, Thorp had been sent out of Bataan by MacArthur in January 1942 with the intent of organizing a resistance movement from among the displaced American units in the Zambales Mountains.

Vicente Bernia paid one of his customary visits to the camp on the morning of August 14. Volckmann seized the opportunity to ask him for a guide to the north as well as any updates on Cayler and Thorp. Since his involvement with the Fassoth Camp, Bernia had kept a close liaison with the other USAFFE personnel in the western provinces. Bernia replied that Cayler was currently outside of Natividad and that Thorp had recently set up his headquarters in the foothills of Mt. Pinatubo. Bernia knew his way around the highland trails to Natividad and gladly offered himself as a guide.

After a four day respite at Bernia's home in the nearby town of Gutad, the Filipino baron led Volckmann, Blackburn, Bruno, and Emilio northward to Natividad. Arriving at the Jincos' home, Blackburn could tell that the family enjoyed taking care of their newfound refugees. Indeed, Cayler and his men were being treated to five meals a day. "The Jinco family was very well-to-do and it amazed me," Blackburn said, "that they took them in and treated them so royally. The Jinco daughters [five in total] prided themselves on their cooking, and I'm telling you, those Chinese gals could really put it on. We stayed two or three days and I hated to leave, because, man they fed us royally! I hadn't tasted food like that even before the war."

Unfortunately, Blackburn knew he couldn't stay there much longer. While finishing another one of their finely cooked meals, Volckmann concluded that "this is wonderful to stay here but it isn't going to be safe for very long." The nearest Japanese garrison was less than twenty miles away and "with all these Americans here, it's bound to draw attention," he said. Plus, Cayler and his men were in no condition for guerrilla warfare. None of them had fully recovered from the beatings they had endured on the Death March. Furthermore, Cayler said that he was awaiting guidance from Thorp, as he had the "last word" on all guerrilla operations in the area. Cayler confided in them, however, that he had lost his confidence in Thorp's leadership. Cayler described him as a snide, condescending, and mercurial leader who had already done more harm than good to the American resistance. He had flippantly dismissed the other Americans in his sector and alienated the local Filipinos.

His biggest mistake, however, had been incurring the wrath of the Hukbalahap. The Hukbalahap, or "Huks," as they were often called, were a combined militia of the Philippine Socialist and Communist Parties. The word *Hukbalahap* was an acronym for *Hukbong Bayan Laban sa mga Hapon* (literally translated: The People's Army Against the Japanese). Before the war, they had denounced the Americans (and wealthy Filipinos like Vicente Bernia) as evil *capitalistas*. But now that they had a common enemy in the Japanese, the Huks had been trying to curry favor with the U.S. military. Blackburn knew that the Huks hadn't suddenly become pro-American, but if he could count on their cooperation for the remainder of the war, they might be useful.

Thorp, however, didn't see it that way. He had solidly rebuffed the Huks and told the "commies" to stay out his business. Cayler's description of Thorp didn't sit well with Blackburn but, if this man truly was the "official" leader of the American resistance, he and Volckmann would have no choice but to submit to his authority. Thanking the Jincos for their hospitality, Blackburn, Volckmann, Bruno, and Emilio reached Claude Thorp's camp on the afternoon of August 20.

When Don Blackburn arrived at Thorp's camp, however, the visit only confirmed what he had heard at Natividad. "Our host was cool, brusque, and condescending," he said. Volckmann explained to Thorp that they were headed for North Luzon and laid out his tentative plans for conducting guerrilla warfare.

Upon hearing this, however, Thorp exploded.

He blasted them as interlopers and asserted that he had been handpicked by the USAFFE leadership to organize the *only* resistance movement in Luzon. Thorp, however, "had failed to demonstrate his capability for the task." Just as Cayler had described, Thorp "had succeeded in alienating both Americans and Filipinos." When asked about Moses and Noble, Thorp's reply was what Blackburn might have expected: they had been through his camp a few weeks earlier and had since gone north.

"After two days of uncompromising and unfruitful discussion," Blackburn said, "we asked for a guide to take us to the Huk headquarters on Mount Arayat, a lone peak that arose from the heart of the Central Plain." It was a risky move soliciting help from the nearby Huks, especially in light of Thorp's undiplomatic behavior, but Blackburn and Volckmann still needed a guide to help them navigate their way through Central Luzon.

Volckmann's inquiry for a guide produced a stocky young native, nicknamed "Kid Muscles," who agreed to take them to the Hukbalahap district headquarters atop Mount Arayat. From there, he said, they could find a guide to take them farther into North Luzon.

On the night of August 24, Blackburn, Volckmann, Bruno, and Emilio departed Thorp's camp with Kid Muscles leading the way. The route to Mount Arayat, however, was extremely dangerous. It took them across the heavily patrolled Highway 11 and passed within sight of Camp O'Donnell, the final destination for those on the Bataan Death March. Saturated with rain and plodding through the muddy trails, the four fugitives finally arrived at Highway 11. Straining their eyes and ears for anything that resembled an enemy truck, the five of them hurriedly dashed across the highway.

Passing by Camp O'Donnell, however, was more unsettling. Atop the guard towers and along the parapets, Blackburn could see the silhouettes of the Japanese guards, pacing back and forth and manhandling their searchlights—anxiously waiting to detect any movement beyond the camp's perimeter. "It was eerie, all lit up," he said, "and we thought about those poor prisoners inside." Kid Muscles hastened the group into a nearby drainage ditch, where the five of them crawled on their bellies below the searching beams of light. As Don shimmied away from Camp O'Donnell, he tried not to think about the atrocities happening within its walls.

"While we were plodding along the rice terraces, and down a road that ran parallel to and below rice fields," Blackburn said, "Russ suddenly nudged me and we saw silhouettes of people on the rice dike." Thinking that it was a Japanese patrol, Volckmann and Blackburn took off running. "Beside us was an old barbed wire fence. I don't know how we got through that barbed wire fence, but it didn't bother us a bit. I was over it and so was he." Kid Muscles took off after them and explained that the silhouettes were Hukbalahap, not Japanese. It had been a Huk patrol that was on its way to raid the Japanese garrison at Santa Rosario.

It was about two o'clock in the morning when Blackburn arrived at the Hukbalahap headquarters. Hiking up the slope of Mount Arayat, he was challenged by the Huk guards every few meters. Using Kid Muscles as an interpreter, they explained that they were Americans seeking help from the Huk leadership. The Huks must have been masters of concealment, Blackburn thought, for although he heard their voices, he never saw a single sentry. Once inside the compound, Blackburn and Volckmann were ushered into the home of the Hukbalahap chieftain, Esuebio Aquino.

Aquino was a man nearly sixty years old, with craggy features and a face weathered by the toils of his proletarian lifestyle. He wasn't bitter about the breakdown with Thorp but was nonetheless disappointed by the man's attitude. Still, he wanted to work with Americans, if for nothing else than to get rid of the Japanese. As Aquino finished his appraisal of the situation, he invited Blackburn and Volckmann to stay at his house and rest for a while. Before retiring to his room, Aquino instructed two of his bodyguards take Blackburn and Volckmann to their guest quarters. Falling asleep on the floor of Aquino's unfurnished guest room, Don Blackburn let out another sigh of relief. He had quietly feared that Hukbalahap would shoot him on the spot. Instead, they were graciously giving him quarters.

Scarcely an hour before dawn, Blackburn was startled awake by the sound of yelling and laughing voices outside his window. It turned out that the same patrol that had frightened him on the way to Mount Arayat had returned from their errand. Sleepy-eyed, Don lumbered outside to see what all the commotion was about. "They were still being led by the girl," he noticed. "She was a beautiful woman . . . the daughter of the mayor of the town of Mexico. The mayor had been killed by the Japs so his daughter joined the guerrillas and was bent on revenge." Indeed, her once-seductive beauty had been replaced by a cold and vengeful countenance. The patrol followed behind her, pushing along a group of prisoners with their hands tied behind their backs. But Don noticed that the prisoners weren't Japanese.

Aquino's son explained that these men were collaborators and were to be executed. Around the corner from Aquino's house was a large boulder which the Huks called Execution Rock. It had earned its name for the public decapitations which had taken place there during the

Spanish rule. Now, Execution Rock was where the Huks meted out their primitive justice. All spies, informants, and collaborators were beheaded with bolo knives. The young girl leading the patrol asked Blackburn if he wanted to attend the execution. He politely declined.

After treating his guests to a hearty breakfast, Aquino instructed one of his men to take them to La Paz, which was as far north as the Huk network extended. The main highway into La Paz, however, was crawling with enemy patrols, so their guide offered to take them through the Candaba Swamp. A few miles into the trip, however, Blackburn began to regret going this way. At the foot of Mount Arayat, he and Volckmann waded into a field of rice paddies. Sinking down to their knees in the stagnant water, this bumbling hike was made worse by the fact that nightfall had come. It was now 7:00 pm and the sun had disappeared behind the swamp's dismal canopy. Their Huk guide, however, kept them at a steady pace, which at times was more trouble than it was worth. Every step seemed to drag them down farther and farther until they stood nearly chest-deep in the swamp ooze.

Luckily, around midnight, the group pulled themselves onto the first slab of dry land that they had seen for miles. There was a settlement nearby, the guide told them, but its inhabitants had been evacuated due to a Japanese patrol that was supposedly targeting Huks in the area. To Blackburn, this sounded ridiculous—why would the Japanese send a patrol into this God-forsaken swamp? He and Volckmann had just spent the past five hours flailing around in this slimy marsh. He couldn't imagine the Japanese taking a foot patrol through here. Reluctantly, though, Don followed the guide to the site where the village had been evacuated. It was a large house just a few miles away that stood prominently on stilts.

After his tribulations through the swamp, Don welcomed the idea of staying inside something that resembled a real house. His enthusiasm, however, quickly soured as he discovered that all seventy-five inhabitants from the evacuated village had been hoarded into the structure. The air inside hung with a heavy stench and the paranoid attitudes of the evacuees didn't make his stay any more enjoyable. But, knowing that he had been through worse, Blackburn stoically huddled himself into a tiny room where he and Volckmann fell asleep.

Sleeping through most of the afternoon, Blackburn, Volckmann, Bruno, and Emilio departed at sundown with a new guide. The rest of

the Canaba Swamp, however, was a lake which required the four of them to travel by native canoe. Their guide, rowing his guests over the bog, took them ashore to the house of an old schoolteacher about one kilometer from La Paz. As the northernmost Huk operative in the area, the old schoolteacher was obviously uncomfortable at the thought of harboring two Americans. It was then that Blackburn discovered that this elderly schoolteacher was an unwilling accomplice in the Huk program—cooperating only because he feared the Hukbalahap more than the Japanese. Then, too, Blackburn knew that the Japanese had built a large garrison in La Paz—the same garrison that had flooded Highway 3 with enemy patrols. With constant pressure from the Hukbalahap, and the lingering threat of Japanese brutality, Don could see why this teacher was so uptight.

Their stay at the old man's house was only slightly better than their previous night's respite. The teacher fed them well but wouldn't let them speak in anything above a whisper. All the shades were drawn tight and their host refused to let them leave the house until dark. As soon as the sun disappeared, he hurried them out of the house, promising to take them to the intersection of Highway 3. Blackburn and Volckmann anticipated a hike of only one hour but the elusive route taken by the schoolteacher added three more hours of trudging through the swamp. The footing was a bit firmer than it had been at the base of Mount Arayat, but Don was quickly growing tired of these swampland expeditions.

Finally arriving at the Highway 3 road junction, the teacher washed his hands of the Americans. Blackburn turned to thank the reluctant Huk, but it was too late—the man had already darted back into the swamp, leaving a trail of rustling leaves and branches in his wake. From there, Blackburn and Volckmann continued up Highway 3, hiding in the barrios by day and travelling the roads by night.

On September 1, Blackburn arrived at barrio Bagabas, where he encountered the first of Robert Lapham's men. Lapham, like Volckmann and Blackburn, was an American officer who had also escaped from Bataan. Lapham had once been under Claude Thorp's command, tasked by the latter to organize guerrillas in the Pangasian Province. Lapham's outfit (the *Luzon Guerrilla Army Force*, as it would later be called) would become one of the best-organized guerrilla operations in Central Luzon.

As it were, Lapham had set up a small network of camps throughout Pangasian, with his headquarters outside of Umingan. According to one of Lapham's men, the Japanese had occupied the same nipa-palm barracks at Umingan where Blackburn's Ilocanos had stayed a few months earlier. When Blackburn and Volckmann arrived at Lapham's, however, he was bed-ridden with a violent fever. Despite his poor health, his camp was well in order and he told Blackburn that Moses and Noble were only a three-day's hike from Umingan.

After breakfast with Lapham on September 4, Blackburn and Volckmann headed north towards San Nicolas where they entered the camp of another American, Charlie Cushing. At Cushing's hideout were two other Americans, Herb Swick and Enoch French, both of whom had worked in the local mining industry. Cushing, meanwhile, told Blackburn that he had last seen Moses and Noble near Bokod in the Benguet sub-province (Mountain Province). He had no further information on their whereabouts, but offered a guide to take them to beyond the Agno River Valley.

Crossing the Agno River with Herb Swick in tow, their guide took them to Lusod, a small barrio named after the nearby mountain. Once there, they met another guerrilla contact named Juan Deleon, a mechanic who had been employed by the local sawmill. According to Deleon, Moses and Noble were just a few hours north, beyond Mount Lusod in a small barrio called Benning. After a two-day respite at Deleon's, Blackburn and the group hit the trail over Mount Lusod and arrived in Benning on September 9, 1942.

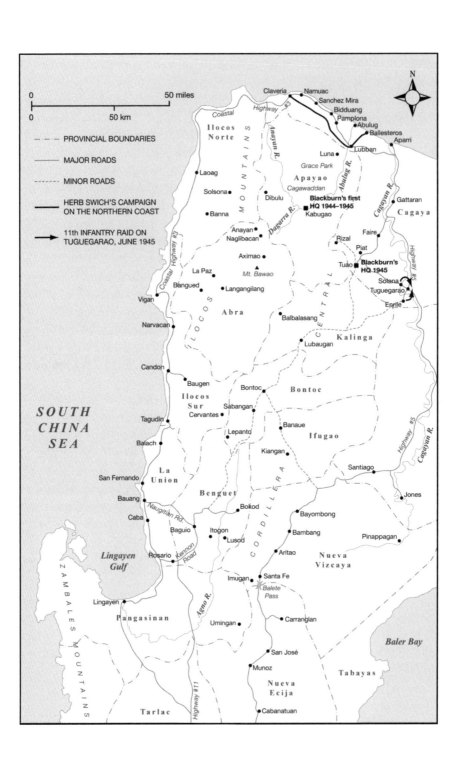

N

0 _____ 50 miles
0 _____ 50 km

–·–·– PROVINCIAL BOUNDARIES

──── MAJOR ROADS

------ MINOR ROADS

──── HERB SWICH'S CAMPAIGN
         ON THE NORTHERN COAST

──▶ 11th INFANTRY RAID ON
         TUGUEGARAO, JUNE 1945

*SOUTH
CHINA
SEA*

Claveria   Namuac
           Sanchez Mira
           Bidduang
           Pamplona
                Abulug
Coastal   Ballesteros
Highway #3   Aparri
Anayan R.
           Luna   Lubban
Grace Park
*Ilocos
Norte*   Apayao
Cagawaddan
      Laoag   Gattaran
   Solsona   Dibulu   **Blackburn's first
                      HQ 1944–1945**   *Cagaya*
      Banna   Kabugao   *Cagayan R.*
      Anayan   Faire
   Naglibacan   Rizal
                            Piat
      Aximao   *Mt. Bawao* Tuao   **Blackburn's
                                    HQ 1945**
   La Paz   Solana
 Bangued   Langangilang   Tuguegarao
Ilocos   Enrile
Vigan   *Abra*
                   Balbalasang
   Narvacan   *Kalinga*
Coastal Highway #3   Lubaugan
      Candon
                            Highway #5
      Baugen   Bontoc   *Bontoc*
   Ilocos   Sabangan
   Sur   Cervantes
   Tagudin   Lepanto   Banaue
   Balach   *Ifugao*
             Kiangan
                        Santiago
   San Fernando   *La
                  Union*
   Bauang   *Naugitian Rd.*   Jones
   Caba   *Benguet*
      Baguio   Bokod   Bayombong
         Itogon Lusod   Bambang
Kennon Road Aritao   Pinappagan
   Rosario   *Nueva
Lingayen   Vizcaya*
Gulf   Imugan   Santa Fe
                    *Balete
ZAMBALES   Pass*
   Lingayen
   Pangasinan Umingan   Carranglan   *Baler Bay*
Agno R.
                    San José   *Tabayas*
                 Munoz
MOUNTAINS   *Nueva
                 Ecija*
Highway #11
   Tarlac   Cabanatuan

CHAPTER 5

NORTH LUZON

B enning was a small native barrio inhabited by the Benguets, a remote tribe of the Igorot people. The news of Blackburn's and Volckmann's arrival in North Luzon had apparently preceded them by a few hours, as Moses and Noble stood at the edge of the settlement with a crowd of natives ready to greet them. It was a joyous reunion and Blackburn was glad to see that the Colonels had made it out of Bataan. For the rest of the afternoon, the fugitives regaled each other with tales of their harrowing escapes. Like before, Martin Moses was calm and reserved. But there was a trace of pessimism in his demeanor—as though he already knew he was on the losing end of his struggle against the Rising Sun. Although he had lost several pounds, he remained in good health, untouched by the tropical diseases which had ravaged many of their comrades. Arthur Noble, too, was in good spirits, although he had lost sight in his left eye. Tragically, the eye had been punctured by a rattan vine during their escape.

With Moses and Noble were Captains Parker Calvert and Art Murphy, both of whom had served under Colonel John P. Horan at Baguio. When Horan surrendered his troops at Baguio and fled to the Zambales Mountains, Calvert and Murphy had remained in the area before meeting up with Moses and Noble that summer. Sitting down to speak with Calvert and Murphy, Don learned the whereabouts of other displaced servicemen who had taken up guerrilla warfare against the Japanese. Most of the information had come from eyewitness accounts or the "bamboo telegraph," a system of native runners who carried information from one town to the next.

According to the "telegraph," Captain George Barnett, who had also served under Colonel Horan, had organized a guerrilla unit on the provincial coasts of Ilocos Norte and Ilocos Sur. Horan himself had been captured at his hideout somewhere in the Zambales Mountains. Horan's capture, however, wasn't the most disappointing piece of news. As a newly minted POW, Horan had broadcast anti-American statements over the Japanese-controlled radio stations and encouraged other USAFFE personnel to surrender. Bando Dagwa, the Philippine Army Reservist and bus company owner who had lent Blackburn his driving manuals, had also formed his own guerrilla unit. Also in the vicinity were Philippine Army Captains Rufino Baldwin, Manuel Enriquez, and Guillermo Nakar.

Enriquez had been in the 71st Infantry under Lieutenant Colonel Bonnett during their retreat across Baguio and down the rocky trails into Aritao. After Bonnett disbanded the retreating column and fled eastward into the Ilongot country, Enriquez and Nakar picked up scattered elements of the 14th Infantry Regiment. After a few months of conducting small-scale raids, however, enemy pressure forced Enriquez and Nakar to split their command: Enriquez took over the western end of Nueva Vizcaya and Benguet, while Nakar moved in to eastern Nueva Vizcaya and Isabela. During this reconsolidation, Nakar had been joined by Captain Robert Arnold, a US Army Signal Corps Officer who had made his way to Isabela from the northern coast of Luzon. The telegraph also told of Captain Ralph Praeger, formerly of the 26th Cavalry (Philippine Scouts), who had formed a small band of guerrillas in the Apayao sub-province. The telegraph also included stories of brave civilians who had taken up the fight against the Japanese. Roque Ablan, the Governor of Ilocos Norte, had foraged a Philippine Army weapons depot and armed his governor's staff, taking them into mountains to conduct guerrilla raids against the Japanese. Perhaps the most notable story was that of Walter Cushing, the American manager of the Luzon-based Rainbow Mining Company. When the Japanese invaded, Cushing armed his workers with guns and bolo knives. Dynamiting bridges and attacking the Japanese columns as they moved southward to Baguio and Manila, Cushing's was the first American-led resistance movement in the Philippines. He was killed by the

Japanese in September 1942, but different versions were told about how he ultimately died. Some reports indicate that he died in a Japanese ambush, cut down by enemy gunfire before he could fire a shot. Other reports suggest that Cushing died in a gun battle at a homestead in Isabela. Whatever the cause of death, the Japanese were so impressed by Cushing's tenacity that they gave him a funeral with full military honors.

Blackburn then turned his attention to Moses and Noble, asking them about their plans for initiating guerrilla warfare. "This Mountain Province was very remote," he later recounted, "with very few roads, and the people were sympathetic towards the US. It was an ideal area in which to initiate some sort of resistance movement." Moses and Noble agreed but did not feel that the time was right, saying that "guerrilla action would be premature" at this point.

The Colonels' response disappointed him. True, the timing may not have been right for direct action, but he thought that Moses and Noble, the senior officers in North Luzon, should have organized *something* by now. As Blackburn retired for the evening, Herb Swick mentioned that there was an American settlement inside Oding, another barrio only a few miles north. According to Swick, the families at Oding were ex-miners and their ranks included a doctor who could help Blackburn with his recurring bouts of malaria. Blackburn, Volckmann, Swick, Bruno and Emilio left for Oding the following morning. When they arrived, the barrio was just as Swick had described it. There were five American families within the settlement and one Filipino doctor. The Americans had worked for the Igoten Mining Company and the Filipino doctor, Dr. Biason, had been the company's staff doctor. Biason had earned his medical degree from the University of Minnesota and was married to an American nurse, Daisy, who was also present at Oding.

Don was deeply impressed by their ingenuity. Each family had built themselves a small wooden house with a galvanized iron roof. Inside each house was an elaborate system of pipes that provided running water from a nearby stream. These families had even created their own power grid. From a generator powered by a nearby water wheel, they had enough electricity for lights and a radio which picked up station KGEI-San Francisco.

Blackburn stayed at Oding from September 10–17. On September

14 he celebrated his twenty-sixth birthday, enjoying a delicious chocolate cake baked by one of the ladies at the camp. At first, Blackburn and Volckmann had planned to make Oding their unofficial "headquarters." However, they soon decided against it. Blackburn and Volckmann knew that if the Japanese discovered their hideout, it would put the American families in jeopardy and force them to move away from the settlement they had worked so hard to build.

On September 15, Herb Swick took Volckmann, Bruno, and Emilio further north to Ekip, a barrio where Swick knew of a good hiding place. Blackburn, however, decided to stay at Oding for a few more days as he was still in need of some malaria shots from Dr. Biason. While recovering at Oding, Don learned from the telegraph that Moses and Noble had moved from Benning to the village of Bobok and had occupied the town's sawmill as their new headquarters. Since Bobok was on the way to Ekip, Blackburn decided to report to Moses and Noble for any updates before meeting Volckmann at Ekip.

At the Bobok sawmill, Moses and Noble informed Blackburn that they had "officially" assumed command of all guerrillas in North Luzon and were planning to launch their campaign on October 15, 1942. Listening to the Colonels, however, Blackburn noticed that their plans lacked any degree of thoroughness. The intended participants were scattered all over North Luzon. And the plan gave no mention to the possibility of enemy reprisals. Blackburn recalled that "there was insufficient time to get messages to the leaders, and then for them to get back to Moses and Noble, and finally, for them to get back to their own organizations and kick things off on D-Day [October 15]. The details for this hadn't been well thought out." Blackburn nonetheless bit his tongue and agreed to pass the information along to Volckmann once he reached Ekip.

Ekip was a three-hour hike from Bobok, most of which was uphill. The tiny barrio stood at an elevation of 6,000 feet, where the temperature was much cooler and rolling clouds provided constant shade from the sunlight. When Don arrived in Ekip, he told Volckmann of his meeting with Moses and Noble at Bobok and delivered their instructions: Blackburn and Volckmann were to meet the Colonels on October 1 to discuss the details of the D-Day operation. Aside from the obvious gaps in the Colonels' planning, Volckmann and Blackburn noticed another problem: the Agno River. During the rainy season, the Agno was wider, deeper, had a stronger current, and provided a natural barrier to the Japanese patrols. Unfortunately, the rains had ended and the Agno was rapidly shrinking to its pre-season size. Furthermore, Blackburn could see the Japanese laying the foundation for a bridge to connect their side of the river to the guerrillas'.

Per orders, Blackburn and Volckmann met with Moses and Noble on October 1, 1942. The counter-offensive was confirmed for October 15 with H-Hour set at 1:00 am. The Colonels' plan was simple: Rufino Baldwin and his men would lead a raid on the Japanese garrison at the Igoten Mines and destroy sections of the Kennon Road to prevent the enemy from reinforcing the area. Baldwin's men were also instructed to capture a Japanese agent named Acota.* Acota had been honchoing things at the Igoten Mining Company for the Japanese and repeatedly gave them information on the whereabouts of guerrilla units. With Acota out of the picture, Moses and Noble hoped to make the Igoten Mines a platform for expanding their guerrilla force.

The night before the raid, Blackburn and Volckmann climbed atop a nearby ridge where they waited for the operation to start. They hoped that the first raid would be a remarkable success. Instead, Don Blackburn and Russ Volckmann saw a tragedy unfold. One of Baldwin's guerrillas prematurely opened fire and forfeited the element of surprise.

What ensued was nearly a total disaster for the USAFFE guerrillas. The Japanese poured out of their garrison and repelled the attack with machine-gun fire. Outclassed by the enemy's automatic weapons, Baldwin's men retreated in panic. To boot, they had missed their opportunity to capture Acota. Alerted by the premature gunfire, Acota ran for cover but, in the ensuing chaos, he had fallen into a nearby ditch where he broke his back. A few of Baldwin's men came upon the helpless figure but soon realized that they could not carry him back to their hideout. Thus, in a fit of panic, they shot Acota where he lay. "Unfortunately, they were [also] recognized by his Filipina mistress, and had to abduct her to prevent her from revealing their identity to the Japs. To make matters worse, she was in the late stages of pregnancy." The very next day, Acota's mistress gave birth to a baby girl and the Japanese began mobilizing reinforcements into the area surrounding the Igoten Mines.

Their punitive expeditions were about to begin.

---

*Other reports have his name spelt as Okoda.

On the morning of October 17, Blackburn returned to Oding to see if Dr. Biason had any more quinine for his relentless malaria. The doctor gladly gave him a shot and told him to spend the next few days in bed. Don rested there until October 24, when Volckmann arrived with more updates from Moses and Noble. Two days earlier, they had gone north to Apayao in hopes of finding Ralph Praeger. It had been reported over the bamboo telegraph that Praeger had acquired a radio transmitter and was in contact with General MacArthur's headquarters in Australia. If the report was true—and Praeger really did have a radio—the Colonels wanted to speak to MacArthur and request further instructions. Sadly, it was the last time Volckmann would ever see Moses or Noble; both men were captured in June 1943.

Also, in the wake of the disastrous raid, Moses and Noble had reformulated their plans for the guerrillas in North Luzon. The Colonels realized that poor communication had been partially to blame for their recent failure at Igoten. As such, they instructed Volckmann and Blackburn to establish a communication center at the abandoned Lusod Sawmill Company, a few miles east of the Igoten Mines. Before the invasion, most of the sawmills in Benguet had been connected through an open-wire telephone circuit. The network had been severely damaged by the Japanese but Blackburn nonetheless began the task of repairing the telephone lines between Lusod and the other sawmills. "The first line that we were going to put up was to run from Lusod, over the Agno River, to Igoten [Rufino Baldwin's camp]. The next line was going to run from Lusod to Bobok [Moses and Noble's HQ]." Blackburn also set up terminals at Bokod and Dalaprit, where Rufino Baldwin's men had recently moved. The way Blackburn envisioned it, the communication network would form a triangle: Baldwin at the first apex, Moses and Noble at the second apex, and he and Volckmann at the third.

The following morning, Blackburn arrived in Bobok to set up a new phone terminal, but found the barrio completely deserted. In his diary, he indicated that Japanese troop movements on the other side of the river had frightened the natives into evacuating.

October 25: We arrived at Bobok around noon and could not find a soul, so proceeded to Cawal barrio where we spent the night. Natives reported that the Japs were at Ambuclao on the opposite bank of the Agno so they had evacuated Bobok. This not confirmed.

October 26. We went to the sitio [another name for barrio] of Benning. I got in touch with a Mr. Gama who had been the electrician for the sawmill at Bobok and arranged a meeting at Lusod on the 27th to discuss plans for the phone net.

October 27. Went to Lusod sawmill. Looked over the remaining house and made arrangements with Juan Deleon, Lusod machinist, to have it repaired for our use.

By Mr. Gama's estimate, it would take about a week to get the Bobok-Lusod phone working again. Later that week, Blackburn decided that Gama and Deleon had been so helpful that they deserved to be inducted into the US Army and put on the guerrillas' payroll. Of course, it was only a symbolic gesture, as neither Blackburn nor Volckmann had the authority to "officially" induct them. But Volckmann promised them that if they rendered their services to the US war effort, they would receive all the rights and privileges of an American GI— and would be compensated accordingly. Volckmann inducted Bruno and Emilio that same day, upon which Bruno gave his real name for the first time, Jose Maddul.

While waiting for the Colonel's next move, Blackburn and Volckmann decided to expand their authority. They sent word to the local barrio leaders instructing them to provide food, firearms, and manpower. It was certainly a bold move: Blackburn and Volckmann had no idea whether the Filipinos would accept their demands. But if they acted like the officers of a defeated army, they would be treated accordingly. They had to convince the Filipinos that the fall of USAFFE and the surrender at Bataan were just "temporary setbacks on the way to inevitable victory."

Luckily, the barrio chieftains responded to their orders quickly and eagerly. They provided the manpower for maintaining the telephone network and accepted IOUs in exchange for rice, vegetables, coffee, and a few cows for meat. Emilio, after slaughtering the cows, put his native talents to good use once again as he showed Blackburn how to clean the meat and make Philippine-style beef jerky. Things continued to go smoothly until Blackburn and Volckmann started getting on each other's nerves.

Whether it was cabin fever, or just the pent-up frustrations of having to evade a ruthless enemy, Blackburn and Volckmann began arguing over trivial matters. For example, the barrio leaders provided the guerrillas with an overwhelming supply of bananas—which Blackburn heartily ate. After finishing his bananas, however, he would throw the peels on the floor of their sawmill headquarters. Blackburn ate so many of them that Volckmann felt overwhelmed by the aroma and the clutter of banana peels. One day, while Blackburn was enjoying another banana, Volckmann's temper finally snapped.

"Christ Almighty, do you have to eat so many of those God-damn bananas?"

"Listen," Don said with a defiant sneer, "I'll eat as many bananas as I please."

Volckmann, perhaps trying to think of a more resentful comeback, replied, "So that's the way you feel about it."

"You're damn right that's the way I feel about it," Blackburn yelled. "This house is too small for the two of us. I'm getting the hell out."

With that, Blackburn stormed out. But he had left Volckmann in such a hurry that he wasn't sure where else he could go. After a moment's thought, he decided to make his way to Oding where he could at least get some more quinine from Dr. Biason. Don's malaria had kept coming back and he was anxious to get rid of it once and for all. Dr. Biason, however, now had something better than quinine. While searching for medical supplies in one of the abandoned sawmills, the doctor had come across three vials of a drug called salvarsan. Normally, salvarsan was used to treatment syphilis, but in recent years, it had also been given to malaria patients. Biason couldn't promise any results, but if it stood a chance of easing the malaria, Blackburn was willing to try it.

Biason delivered the drug intravenously and, within a day, Blackburn reported feeling better than he had in months. His temper had also calmed down enough to return to the sawmill he shared with Volckmann. When he returned to their Lusod hideout, however, he was shocked to see Volckmann building a crib. With a smile, Volckmann explained that he had agreed to take care of Mrs. Acota and her baby.

"Mrs." Acota, however, was a difficult woman to read. She didn't care much for either the Americans or the Japanese, and even though she had been Acota's common-law wife, she didn't seem the least bit upset by his sudden death. Blackburn and Volckmann never gave many details about her, but by virtue of being Acota's mistress, they knew she had close ties to the Japanese leadership. All things considered, it was better to keep her in custody than risk her becoming another informant.

Since her newborn baby needed milk, Blackburn and Volckmann went north to Sumulpuss to speak to the barrio chieftain. Using Bruno as an interpreter, the barrio chief said that he regrettably had no more cows, but he did have a goat. Since goat milk was better than none, Blackburn agreed to take the animal. The barrio leader, however, added one condition: there would have to be an armed guard assigned to Mrs. Acota at all times. The barrio leader was afraid that Mrs. Acota already knew too much about the resistance movement. Therefore, if she tried to escape, the guard would eliminate her, lest she report their activities to the Japanese. Cruel as it may have sounded, Blackburn knew that such measures were necessary for self-preservation.

By November 9, the phone lines had been completed and their camp at Lusod was well in order. Blackburn and Volckmann's staff now included Bruno, Emilio, Juan Deleon, a young native guide named Atong, and Tenny, the elderly native woman who had become the guerrilla's master chef. Unfortunately, Blackburn and the others would not enjoy their Lusod camp for very long. "We were in the process of establishing this communications net, locating where people were, and passing information to Moses and Noble, when things began to disintegrate." November 9, 1942 marked the beginning of the Japanese counteroffensive.

As the Agno River returned to its smaller size, Blackburn recalled that the Japanese "moved en masse out of Baguio and into the hills [of Benguet sub-province]. They were often led by Filipinos [informers] who knew the trails throughout the area where we were operating. And from November 1942 until the following August 1943, the Japs were constantly mopping up the mountains and the coastal areas."

On the morning of November 10, the guards from Sumulpuss took Mrs. Acota back to their barrio while Volckmann, Blackburn, Bruno, and Emilio took shelter in an abandoned hut about 1,000 yards up the mountainside. "That same night," Blackburn said, "they [the Japanese] camped right below us on the slope. . . . they knew we were at the sawmill." Looking down the mountain and into the countryside, Blackburn could see the enemy everywhere. Their tents and company flags dotted the landscape. And just beyond the horizon, he could see trails of smoke, ostensibly from the enemy campfires.

Blackburn and the others stayed atop their mountain hideout for three more days, during which time he could hear the Japanese marching along the trails only a few yards below him. Luckily, dense fog and heavy foliage near the summit kept Blackburn well hidden from his pursuers. After the third day, the Japanese called off their search and retreated down the mountain. Don and others waited for a day to make sure they were gone before heading back to Sumulpuss. Once there, however, the natives delivered some disheartening news: Mrs. Acota had escaped with her baby and had somehow evaded her native guards. Disgusted, Blackburn knew that it was a matter of time before this turncoat mistress reported him to the Japanese. "That night, we took off and headed for the Mountain sub-province of Ifugao, one of the five Igorot sub-provinces that comprised Mountain Province." Benguet had become a hornet's nest and Blackburn knew that it was no place to continue his guerrilla operations. Fortunately, Bruno was a native of Ifugao and many of his relatives were barrio leaders there. Using his family connections, Bruno could cash in a few favors to provide the group with food, weapons, and loyal manpower.

First, however, the group decided to stop by Oding to see how the American families had fared throughout the Japanese reprisals. As Blackburn got closer to the American camp, however, they could see the footprints of the Japanese's hobnail boots. Alarmed at the sight of the enemy footprints, Blackburn and the others increased their gait to a full sprint until they staggered into Oding—or rather, what was left of it.

Just as he had feared, the Japanese had burned the houses to the ground. Clothes, furniture, and various other household items had been scattered everywhere and there was no sign of Dr. Biason or the American miners. "We didn't tarry long at Oding," Blackburn said. "There was nothing to keep us around the area, so we pushed on towards Ifugao." Blackburn later discovered that only two of the five families at Oding had escaped. The other three, along with Dr. and Mrs. Biason, had been captured and thrown into a prison camp.

The next day's hike took them through the Taboy River Valley, where no white man had ever been before. Their descent into the Taboy

Valley brought them in contact with the most primitive tribes they had met. These natives were herders who had no reservations about sharing their homes with—and sleeping next to—their livestock. Unlike the barrio-dwellers, these natives made no attempt at personal hygiene and their dialect sounded more like a series of grunts. Their speech was so incoherent that even Bruno, Blackburn's ace interpreter, had difficulty understanding them. Sifting through the words of their guttural dialect, Bruno discovered that these natives knew nothing about the invasion or the Japanese. "Japanese? No, they had never seen any of them—who were they? It was incredible. Apparently, this part of the Taboy Valley was so uninviting that even the backwash of war had avoided it."

As their hike through the upper Taboy Valley continued, Blackburn's malaria relapsed yet again. And, as he had come to expect with each recurring bout, his strength began collapsing. Bruno, however, informed the group that the Nungawa barrio was a day's hike away and the barrio lieutenant was his cousin. Begrudgingly, Volckmann turned to Blackburn and said, "We're going to move whether you're sick or not!" Volckmann hated seeing his friend hobble down the trail, but knew that they needed to get to Nungawa. The longer they remained in the open, the more vulnerable they were to the Japanese and their fifth column stooges. When the group finally arrived at Nungawa, Blackburn collapsed. Rushing him into the barrio lieutenant's home, Volckmann appealed for help. Fortunately, Bruno's cousin made their stay at Nungawa enjoyable: "They put us up, fed us and took care of us for several days."

Blackburn also recalled that "Bruno's father, then deceased, had been a tribal chief of the Ifugaos, so Bruno's family was prominent in the area. It was decided to put us in a little hut that was on the side of the hill above the barrio which was concealed by tall cogon grass." And the grass certainly was tall—it grew over ten feet high. Bruno's cousin also designated people to bring food to Blackburn and Volckmann instead of having them go into the barrio to get it.

On the first day at Nungawa, Blackburn and his friends were greeted as heroes wherever they went. He was amazed at how much faith these natives had placed in the Americans and how much the Filipinos preferred them over the Japanese. The news of their arrival in Ifugao obviously spread fast because "things started happening right after we got there," Blackburn said. "There were a lot of Philippine

Scouts and Philippine Constabulary in the area who had their weapons. We began getting a flood of these people coming to see us. These were well-trained personnel who had refused to surrender and were evading capture." Blackburn and Volckmann were delighted. Despite the fury of the Japanese campaign, there were still those who remained loyal to the American cause.

By the one-year anniversary of Pearl Harbor, Blackburn and Volckmann had established a new camp outside Kiangan. This "camp" was little more than a small hut, but he and Blackburn made it livable by building beds and making a carpeted floor sewn together from cogon grass.

While awaiting orders from Moses and Noble, December was fairly quiet. Blackburn received no further enemy contact and spent most of his time regrouping from the previous month. He nonetheless busied himself with some light exercise to stave off the malaria. The following diary entries close out Blackburn's first year of the war:

December 9. Rained all day. The Japs are making life tougher every day as they get better organized. They have spies everywhere, which makes it very difficult to move around.

December 10. Built a bed today out of runo grass. Now we don't have to sleep on the floor. The Japs in Kiangan are having clean-up week. They are forcing the surrounding barrios to furnish men to clear the thick underbrush within a one-kilometer radius of town. Evidently, they don't want guerrillas sneaking up on them.

December 14. Another horrible day. Rain and nothing to read. Have been getting books from Mr. Herrin [the local minister of a Unitarian Church] and the lady missionaries [these were American missionaries Lottie Spessard, Myrtle Metzger, and another identified only as "Mrs. Kluge"] but have read them all. I can feel malaria creeping up on me again so have started another five-day course on quinine supplied by the lady missionaries, fifteen grains a day. I have found that if I catch the malaria soon enough, I can stop it.

Ended our day with the usual topic—wonder what MacArthur is doing? Bruno went to Mr. Famorca's store and returned with some purico (lard) and some coconuts [Famorca was a local merchant whom Volckmann had put on the guerrilla payroll]. He also brought some news from Mr. Herrin: American planes bombed the island of Leyte. I hope that this is true.

December 21. Three more shopping days before Christmas. Received sugar, purico, salt and cigars from the merchant Famorca in Kiangan. Atong and Bruno brought home a calf tonight, our first meat in a long time.

December 22. Spent the day butchering the calf. Sent one front quarter to Mr. and Mrs. Herrin, the liver and the other front quarter to the missionaries. We'll smoke and dry the rest. T-bone steak for dinner.

December 23. Tried our hand at sausage making with Emilio leading the experiment. We chopped the meat up fine, funneled it into a bag made from the skin of the calf's intestines, then tied up the open end. It worked. Then we put the sausage in the chimney and smoked it.

Christmas Eve. "Twas the night before Christmas and all through the house, not a creature was stirring, not even a mouse." We don't have mice, they're rats and they'll be raising hell soon, as usual. The second unhappy Christmas in a row. Mother and Dad must be wondering and worrying—I only wish that I could let them know that I am alive. Ann is on my mind constantly.

Christmas Day. A rainy, disagreeable morning. The gloom still prevails but we have much to be thankful for. We are thankful that we haven't been captured—and we don't intend to be. I would rather be dead than half-dead in a Japanese prison camp. More radio news from Mr. Herrin: "Our troops are in Borneo; Baguio has been bombed."

We can't rely on this. These people bring in the darndest news and if you check up on it you'll find that about nine-tenths of it just isn't so. And to find out it isn't true is quite a letdown. Moral: don't listen to rumors.

December 28. Bruno brought in some snap beans, mustard greens, field peas and camotes. Heard from Mr. Herrin that Italy has been occupied and that 250,000 troops have arrived in China. Sounds great, but is it true?

December 30. I chopped a tree and read *A Tale of Two Cities*. Heard from Mr. Herrin that one million American troops have landed in China. This represents a considerable increase over his last estimate.

December 31. Took a walk to the top of mountain to look around. It was the kind of day that makes you feel good; the air was clear, the sun was bright and warm. The country below looked very peaceful with the natives working their wonderful rice terraces. I returned home about 1100 and enjoyed a segundo almuerzo [mid-day snack] of coffee and cookies. Bruno came in with a bottle of tapoy [rice wine] with which we will celebrate New Year's Eve.

CHAPTER 6

AGAINST THE TIDES

Throughout the spring and summer of 1943, Blackburn and Volck-mann did what they could to organize the guerrillas in North Luzon. It was certainly no easy task. In response to the raid on the Igoten Mines, the Japanese launched their first cohesive anti-guerrilla campaign of the war. But what Blackburn found odd was the inconsistent nature of the Japanese Army's counterinsurgency. Through one side of their mouths, the enemy would say things like "peace and tranquility," encouraging Filipinos to accept the "new order" and join them in the Greater East Asia Co-Prosperity Sphere, where they could be free of American influence. Through the other side of their mouths, however, the Japanese would give orders to rape, pillage, and burn entire villages if they suspected any support for the American guerrillas. Adding further to Japanese duplicity was a proclamation saying any Americans who surrendered now would not be treated as "bandits," but as "prisoners of war." To Don Blackburn, however, the distinction was dubious. He was well aware of the atrocities happening within the prison camps. Whether "bandit" or POW, any American would be treated about the same.

The Japanese also enacted a "Plan of Propaganda," which used local leaders and "puppet" officials to urge the surrender of those who were still in hiding. One such puppet was the Mayor of Kiangan. What made him so troublesome, however, was that his allegiance would change with the tides: one day he was decidedly pro-American, the next day, pro-Japanese. But what angered Blackburn more than shifting loyalties were the lies circulated by the Japanese-controlled media. Around the clock, the Japanese ran broadcasts of their so-called "victory" and how Asians were racially superior to the "white imperialist dogs" of the West. America had been beaten, they said, and she would never return to the Pacific. The Filipinos' only chance for prosperity, therefore, was to join hands with the Japanese. But then again, the Japanese's brutality did little to help their propaganda machine.

Meanwhile, Blackburn and Volckmann settled on a "lay low" strategy. Candidly, it was the only choice they had. The Japanese counterinsurgency was running at full steam and their friends in the fifth column still lurked behind every bend. As for Moses and Noble, they hadn't been seen or heard from since embarking on their manhunt for Ralph Praeger. Still, Blackburn and Volckmann decided to use their downtime wisely. If and when the Colonels returned, Volckmann and Blackburn wanted to have a sizeable guerrilla force ready for action.

That January, Blackburn inducted another Filipino named Basilio Tayaban. He was a product of the US missionary schools and had a fairly good command of the English language. Blackburn described him as having "more guts than sense," but his eagerness to fight the Japanese won him a spot on the American team. Another eager recruit who showed up at the Kiangan camp was Alfredo Bunnol. Like Emilio, Alfredo had been a Sergeant in the Philippine Constabulary who refused to join the ranks of the Japanese flunkies.

February 6: The Mayor of Kiangan made a speech in the barrio below us this morning in which he announced the forming of neighborhood associations. These neighborhood associations are not to turn in soldiers but to see that the soldiers are well fed and send them on their way. I hope the old boy is sincere when he says that he will do his best to cover up the soldiers who will not surrender.

February 8: [The duplicitous mayor changes hats again] The Mayor of Kiagan made a speech this afternoon in which he said that he was asking the [Philippine] Scouts of Banaue and Burney to surrender and that he would go with them to Bontoc. He said that the Japs have promised independence to the Philippines if all the soldiers surrender soon.

February 14: Ann's birthday. I wish we were celebrating it together. Bruno and his friend Lumlum showed up today with a radio. But what will we use for electricity? We need a battery, a generator for charging the battery and a bicycle gear with which to work the generator. Bruno and Lumlum also brought me a Springfield rifle which is in terrible shape.

February 16: This is the day the Japs have set as the surrender-allegiance deadline. After today any soldier who has not signed up will be shot if caught.

February 19: Spent the day reading *Thirty Years with the Philippine Head-Hunters*. Its author, Samuel E. Kane, an American governor of the Mountain Province, says that the Ifugaos make wonderful marksmen. As soon as we can get our hands on enough guns, we'll see if Kane is right.

On February 26, three more Philippine Scouts reported for duty: Francisco Balanban, Antonio Guiniling, and Joaquin Timbuloy. Balanban was the leader of the group and already had a sizeable guerrilla force under his wing—fifteen Scouts, all of whom still had their Garand rifles.

Meanwhile, Volckmann began looking beyond Ifugao to garner support from the other tribes in Mountain Province. Just beyond the valley from Volckmann and Blackburn's camp lay the Haliap tribe. According to the Ifugao, the Haliap were a primitive clan of headhunting savages. Their leader, Kamayong, had a reputation as the most fearsome warrior in Mountain Province. If Kamayong and his men were indeed as fearsome as described, then Volckmann had no doubt that the Haliap would make good guerrillas.

Before soliciting help from the Haliap, Blackburn and Volckmann consulted with Tamicpao, chief of the Antipolo tribe. Blackburn said that "he was considered by everyone around there to be the most powerful native chief in the area." Indeed, Tamicpao was a vigorous man and he looked decades younger than his 70 years would suggest. "Tamicpao did not beat around the bush. He said he would do everything in his power to support the guerrillas," and even offered to let them build more camps in the Antipolo territory. Blackburn was grateful to have gained his support.

March 11: Almost every day now we send small groups of men

on trips over the mountains to recruit guerrillas, keep in touch
with those already organized, and check on enemy movements.
This morning, Basilio Tayaban and a squad of four left on a
trip that will take about two weeks.

March 12: It's been a long time since we've had authentic
news. Every day we wonder how much longer we'll have to lead
this underground life. It's been a long grind, but if our health
holds up, we'll make it.

I think of Ann too much, wondering if she'll wait for me. I
hope she has the courage and faith to hold on, but it's been over
a year since she last heard from me. Under these circumstances
it's too bad I love her so much although it's the thought of her
that gives me the determination to keep fighting until I see her
again.

The Japs have proclaimed March 19–22 as fiesta time. Each
family must contribute money, rice, and vegetables. The people
are very angry. This kind of thing makes them want the Americans to come back to the Philippines. For people say that when
the Americans were here they gave the fiesta and bore the
expense, enabling the poor to eat meat, an opportunity they
seldom have. The people also say that when the Americans were
here everyone had a chance to work and earn money. Now
there is no work except for forced labor at no pay. If only American planes would fly over and drop leaflets once in a while
emphasizing these points in our favor and promising the return
of our armies.

March 19: I am leaving tomorrow on a reconnaissance
patrol, taking three men with me [Bruno and two other Ig-
orots]. I want to look the country over, talk to the people, pick
sites for future camps, and see an American guerrilla named
Fish, whom I plan to meet at Ekip. I hope my malaria holds off
during this trip.

Blackburn also wanted to see how things had progressed in Benguet. It had been a few months since the chaos of the previous fall had
forced him and Volckmann into Ifugao. He wanted to know if any
Americans remained in the sub-province and get any updates on the
Japanese activity there.

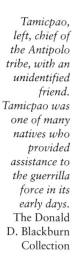

Tamicpao, left, chief of the Antipolo tribe, with an unidentified friend. Tamicpao was one of many natives who provided assistance to the guerrilla force in its early days. The Donald D. Blackburn Collection

When Blackburn arrived in Ekip, however, he was greeted with a cascade of bad news. The enemy activity hadn't quieted down at all. Herb Swick, who had chosen to stay in Benguet, had been captured; Parker Calvert and Art Murphy were on the run, and Charles Cushing had deserted his camp.

Fish, however, was free and in good spirits.

Fish been a lumberman before the war and had been conducting guerrilla operations in Benguet for some time. He knew of some friendly elements that remained in the area despite the recent fury, and offered his camp as a relay station in the growing communication network. According to Fish, the Japanese had devastated the province, but there were enough friendly outposts left in Benguet to form small cadres for the guerrilla force.

The 9th of April was a bitter day for Volckmann and Blackburn— the one-year anniversary of the American surrender at Bataan. In his diary, Blackburn wrote:

> April 9: A date I'll never forget; a year ago today, Bataan fell. When Russ and I think back on it, we still rejoice that we decided to escape rather than surrender, although we had no idea of the hardships that lay in wait for us. Nor did we have any conception of the love and loyalty we would receive from the Filipinos.
>
> It will be a great day when we can walk in the open again and feel relatively safe. When we travel now in daylight, we use trails known only to the guerrillas. And our loaded revolvers are always within reach even when we sleep.
>
> April 15: In the morning good news on the "bamboo telegraph": Moses and Noble have reached Praeger and used his radio. They sent word to the War Department via Australia that as of March 23, 1943, we were safe and free on Luzon. Now Dad and Mother and Ann will have something to hope on.
>
> The report from Moses and Noble also passed on the strategy [MacArthur's] headquarters wants [them] to follow with their guerrilla force. It is pretty much what we have already put into effect: "to cease active operations against the enemy; to concentrate on gathering and collecting intelligence of enemy dispositions and activities and transmit same to headquarters; to keep up the people's morale; and to perfect organization and plans for action at a later date."

Around this time—despite admonitions from the Ifugao residents— Blackburn and Volckmann decided to consult with Kamayong and the dreaded Haliap tribe. Meeting Kamayong for the first time, however, Don discovered that his appearance belied his fearsome reputation. For the most feared headhunter in the Igorot country, Kamayong stood barely over five feet tall. "You could hardly believe he could scare anybody," Blackburn recalled. Much to their surprise, they also found the Haliap chief to be a charming and pleasurable man. As leader of the Haliap, he assured Blackburn that his land was safe for the guerrillas' use. He even offered to let them build their new headquarters in his tribal lands.

Kamayong thought that Volckmann and Blackburn were too fenced-in by the cogon-concealed huts in Antipolo. Plus, Kamayong didn't feel that the Antipolo could guarantee their safety in the manner he could. The Haliap leader kept a close eye on his people, and his influence over them was strong. Also, the trails throughout the region were sparse, and often only the Haliap knew their locations. Hence, Volckmann decided to establish his new headquarters in the Haliap lands of Ifugao. The Halip headquarters then became Camp One, and their Antipolo base became Camp Two.

April 18: Instead of being on the run, we have been given sanctuary that seems the most secure that we have so far encountered. The mountains around us are covered with thick green growth and in addition to the concealment given by nature, there is a protective wall provided by the Haliap barrios which surround us. In each of these barrios, Kamayong has men who will warn us if the enemy comes near.

Kamayong is an extraordinary leader. His word is law in Haliap. If Kamayong is your friend, his followers are your friends. Around noon today the Haliaps began coming to see us, bearing tokens of their friendship, baskets of food, and bottles of tapoy [rice wine]. The Haliap guards never leave us but squat on the ground grinning, in their bare feet and G-strings, with their razor-sharp bolos always within reach.

Kamayong keeps in close touch with his people and does not allow those feuds to develop that cripple some Igorot communities. All his people sing his praises. He is kind and just to them but he can be hard on those who get out of line.

April 20: Now that we are reasonably safe, we can devote some more time to our organization. Russ, Bruno, and Basilio Tayaban made a trip to our camp at Pula, Antipolo, to see how the men were getting along.

Russ reported that our men who are not out on patrol have found a new way to finance our army. They are weaving baskets and chicken coops out of rataan and selling them in Antipolo.

We call Haliap Camp One, and the one [in Antipolo], Camp Two. We plan to establish a third camp which we will use just for storing arms and records. We hope to establish Camp Four on the southern border of Ifugao, adjacent to the territory more or less controlled by the guerrilla leader Enriquez. We should have one more camp in the Taboy river valley to solidify the entire area and keep hostile people from entering it. Such are the plans we hope to carry out in the near future.

April 22: We have been given a radio that works. Now the problem is to find a way to charge the battery.

Yesterday two Haliap women return from Kiangan and spread the story around the barrio that the Japs had arrested a man in Kiangan. When Kamayong heard about this he sentenced the women to ten days' hard labor on the new school [a local building project]. He does not allow his people to talk about either Japs or Americans. Spreading rumors in Haliap is a misdemeanor.

Listened to KGEI, San Francisco, last night. Nothing astounding on the radio.

These simple people of the mountains are the most loyal to the United States. As simple as they are, they realize what the Americans have done for them and they appreciate it. There are very few pro-Japs among them. Most of the pro-Japs in Mountain Province are displaced lowlanders, Tagalogs and Ilocanos. For the sake of these pagans, who appreciate anything done to help them, who are the most loyal people on Luzon, who turned out to be the best in the Philippine Army—I hope the United States continues to exert its influence in the Philippines. All these people tell us that they do not want the Americans to leave, that the Americans have helped them immeasurably by opening schools, building roads and bridges, and providing ways to earn a little money.

April 25: Some bad news over the bamboo telegraph this morning. Captain Rufino Baldwin was captured near the Igoten Mine; Lieutenant Charles Cushing was captured. Enriquez surrendered. Our group is getting smaller and smaller.

In the late afternoon Kamayong came by with his son, Pardo, and the treasurer of Haliap, Jerauldo, to listen to the radio news. It sounded a little bit better. The English, French, and Americans are making a drive on Tunis in North Africa. First we've heard of the Americans in some time.

April 26: The battery of our radio gave out before we got the news. I hope we can get a water wheel working soon.

April 30: Kamayong and Jerauldo came for lunch. They went to the celebration in Kiangan yesterday. The Japanese commanding officer told the people that the war was over and the United States defeated. The Japs put out this propaganda along with any kind of story they think the ignorant will believe. For instance, a citizen of Kiangan came up to Kamayong and told him that if any Americans were hiding in the mountains, the Japs could easily find them because they have a secret hearing device which enables them to detect and trace "American noises." Just what are "American noises?" The Bronx cheer?

May 2: The Japs held a meeting of Igorot women. The Jap officer spokesman asked, "When the Spanish were here, the Filipinos like the Spaniards. Why?" The Igorot women answered, "Because they brought us religion."

The Jap asked, "When the Americans were here, you liked the Americans. Why?" The answer was, "Because they taught us to read and write."

The Jap then asked, "Why don't the Filipinos like the Japanese?" A woman answered, "Because the Japs are cruel and kill Filipinos."

That broke up the meeting.

The rest of May passed without much incident, but the most devastating blow to the North Luzon guerrillas, occurred on June 1, 1943—Moses and Noble were captured in Kalinga. They were returning from Praeger's hideout in Apayao, and while traveling towards Lubuagan the Colonels had taken ill and sought refuge in a cave not far from a native barrio. After sending one of their men into the barrio for any medical relief, he was intercepted by a Japanese patrol. True to form, the Japanese tortured the man until he broke down and gave the exact location of the Colonels' hiding place.

Apprehended and beaten, Moses and Noble were sent to Bontoc

where the Japanese garrison commander forged a surrender order with
the Colonels' names attached:

Bontoc, Mt. Province
Philippine Islands
June 9, 1943
Special Orders

1. I surrendered for the peace and happiness of the Philippines
   to the forces of the Imperial Japanese Army in Kalinga on
   June 2, 1943. Since our surrender we have been treated with
   kindness and generosity and in every case according to the
   Rules of the International Law.
2. I have been assured by officials of the Imperial Japanese
   Army that all members of the USAFFE still at large on
   Luzon, who surrender now, will be treated in the same way
   and in no case will any of them be tortured or killed.
3. All members of the USAFFE now at large on Luzon are,
   therefore, hereby "AT ONCE" to surrender to the Bontoc
   Garrison of the Imperial Japanese Army.
4. We will pray to God for your happiness and peaceful life.

> Signed: Martin Moses [signature]
> Martin Moses [typed]
> Lt. Col. Infantry, U.S. Army
> Commanding
>
> Witness: Arthur Noble [signature]
> Arthur Noble [typed]
> Lt. Colonel, Infantry, U.S. Army

CHAPTER 7

CAGAYAN VALLEY

For all their good intentions, Moses and Noble had done little
more than send the Allied resistance further into chaos. Thus,
Volckmann and Blackburn began the arduous process of organizing
the guerrillas scattered about North Luzon. It was an excruciatingly
slow process fraught with betrayals, intrigue, manhunts, and the inevitable close calls with the Japanese. But nonetheless, Don Blackburn
and Russ Volckmann made it work.

Before they could get underway, however, they had another problem on their hands: a Japanese patrol was on its way to Haliap.

June 20. Russ and Bruno returned from Camp Two and in a
cheerful mood over lunch decided that the Japs would not
bother us for some time.

The cheerful mood didn't last long. After lunch, Chupig
[another guerrilla from Haliap] came running up, crying that
the Japs were in the barrio right below us, not forty-five minutes away. We packed pell-mell and moved everything to the
"evacuation hut" in the jungle, then we went back and waited
with our guns ready. We wanted to be sure that this wasn't just
another false report.

After a while word came from Kamayong that the report
was true; the Japs were heading for Haliap. The hideout we had
prepared was only about an hour's walk from our house, but

91

the darkness caught up with us. It rained all the way and the path we took through the jungle was a hunter's trail covered with leeches. If it weren't for the guides we would have floundered around in the jungle all night.

June 21. We sent Pedro to Haliap this morning to check on the Japs: the Japs are still in Haliap. We heard a big flight of bombers overhead but couldn't see them because the roof of the jungle is so thick. We sent Pedro back for some more news and posted a guard on the trail.

June 22. Pedro returned around noon. The Japs left Haliap early this morning . . . we will stay here for a couple of days just to make sure they're out of range.

June 23. Still in our jungle hideout, a one-room shack barely big enough for all six of us to squeeze in out of the rain.

June 24. We figured that the enemy was far enough away so we moved back home and spent the day drying out damp clothes, oiling our guns, and in general straightening out the mess.

Returning to their camp, Don learned that during their patrol the Japanese hadn't asked any questions, nor had they fired a single shot. Blackburn wasn't sure what the Japanese were up to, but whatever the reason for their uneventful patrol, they were gone now. It was time to get back to work.

June 26. Around eleven Bruno and I went to Camp Two. We found Atong waiting for us with the water wheel and generator from Oding. He had heard over the bamboo telegraph that the Japs were in Haliap and decided to remain in Antipolo.

June 27. We have sent a stern warning to the pro-Jap councilor of Cawayan. We heard he was gathering information about guerrillas for the Japs. We warned him that if this were so he and his family would pay with their lives. He sent word back quickly that it was not so. We are having to watch him constantly.

June 29. Malaria again. Started on quinine. Hope I caught it in time to knock it out in a few days.

July 6. I have been sick as a dog for a week with chills, high fever and aches all over my body. This time the quinine didn't catch up to the malaria. Today at last, I felt considerably better. Russ has been on the sick list too.

The Japs in Kiangan are quiet and are said to be convinced after their pleasant, peaceful visit to Haliap, that this area is free of guerrillas.

July 16. Basilio returned from Camp Two with a big bundle of messages from the following: Fish, George Barnett, Parker Calvert, Bando Dagwa, Dennis Molintas and Manriquez. Fish's message stated that a large patrol of Japs is marching around Benguet looking for Blackburn and Volckmann. As long as they look for us down there it's O.K.

July 21. Sergeant Alfredo Bunnol brought his patrol back from Benguet. He reported that area crawling with spies and informers, many of whom are apparently looking for Major Volckmann and Captain Blackburn. We are still impressed by Bunnol's leadership qualifications. We need good Filipino officers. If Bunnol works out, we'll put him in charge of the camp we plan to establish in Annayao's territory.

By August 1, 1943, the guerrillas' supply system was in the best shape it had ever been. Volckmann had opened up several lines of credit in Manila and Baguio with merchants who were friendly to the Allied cause. However, August also brought its share of sorrow. On the 8th of the month, Blackburn learned the fate of Enoch French, the comrade whom he had met at Cushing's camp with Herb Swick. As it turned out, French had somehow procured a printing press and begun printing counterfeit Japanese money. At first it seemed like a good idea—French would no longer have to keep track of any IOUs. However, his actions had an unintended consequence when the counterfeiting led to inflation in the local market. One day, French's bodyguard, Pedro Velasco, asked French for some money to fund his upcoming wedding. French happily gave him two hundred dollars of the counterfeit currency. Normally, in the Philippine economy of the 1940s, French's sum would have been more than enough to cover the costs. But since he had flooded the market with counterfeit notes, it was hardly sufficient. Velasco demanded more money, but when French refused Velasco shot him. Having killed Enoch French, Velasco sought refuge with the Japanese and defected to their Bureau of Constabulary.* Nonetheless, the Benguet guerrillas avenged French's death by setting an ambush for Velasco and one of his Constabulary patrols.

Blackburn also found out that Rufino Baldwin had been captured and interned at Fort Santiago. However, August ended on a brighter note with the commissioning of Alfredo Bunnol and Francisco Balaban. Both were promoted from sergeant to lieutenant. Blackburn noted that Balaban was well liked by his men but Bunnol was the stronger tactician.

> August 21. Moses and Noble are still alive and are being held prisoner at Baguio. They were allowed to make a speech over the radio, apparently in the belief that they would appeal to their fellow Americans to surrender. But when they got in front of the microphone, they sent out this message before being cut off the air: "Keep up your spirits, it won't be long now. The offensive is just around the corner."

During the first week of September, Blackburn and Volckmann made their rounds inspecting the camps they had established and visiting more barrios. Frequenting such hamlets as Aliwang and Pitol, Blackburn found the same warm reception he had seen in other parts of Ifugao. The barrio chieftains welcomed them with open arms and feasts of the finest native fare they could muster. Blackburn was pleased as he knew that gaining the civilians' support was the first step in maintaining a successful guerrilla force.

> September 14. I am wishing myself a happy birthday at the age of twenty-seven. I hope that sooner or later I can celebrate another birthday in the United States.
> September 15. Kamayong came up for a visit and reported that the Japs have promised to give the Philippines their independence on September 20th—but who believes them?
> September 17–21. Rain

*The Bureau of Constabulary had been established by the Japanese after the fall of Bataan. It was a domestic security force made of Filipino conscripts. Although some accepted their conscription without complaint, most did so only out of fear.

September 24. News from Benguet about the outside world: the tides of the war have definitely turned in Europe. Perhaps they will change soon in Luzon.

September 29. A runner arrived with alarming news—the Japs are just below us in a barrio only twenty minutes away. We packed hurriedly, and moved everything but our packs and bunks to our jungle hideout, a cave cleared out by Bruno and Emilio. One of the Haliaps went to check on the enemy movements and report back to us.

October 1. We catnapped in our cave hideout with the Japs just half an hour away. The night was clear and cold and most of our bedding was packed and hidden. Around five in the morning, the Haliap we had sent to watch the Japs returned to report that the enemy is going to remain . . . and question Councilor Kamayong. The information on which the enemy is working comes from a guerrilla who recently surrendered.

October 2. The Japs left, taking their informer with them. We moved back into our house.

October 3. Kamayong came up and reported that the Japs asked about us but apparently knew very little except our names. They are now in Antipolo en route to Tenuc looking for Major Manriquez who happens to be about two hundred miles away, Pangasian.

October 4. Basilio came in from Camp Two and reported that the Jap patrol asked about us. They learned nothing definite, but the situation is unhealthy; there are too many spies and informers around. We are making plans to eliminate some of them, one in particular who lives in a barrio just below Camp Two.

October 7. Dennis Molintas arrived. He is a former school teacher, a soft-spoken man about forty years old. Molintas and Bando Dagwa, who owned the bus company in Baguio, organized a guerrilla unit, which they led into Parker Calvert's force. Calvert's headquarters are at Kapangan, Benguet, about ten miles north of Baguio.

During the meeting with Dennis Molintas, Volckmann announced his reorganization of the North Luzon guerrilla force. At present, Volckmann wanted to focus on expanding the force, training, and building confidence with small-scale raids, ambushes and sabotage missions before US conventional forces returned to Luzon. From what Volckmann could estimate, there were four regimental commands left in the area. These included remnants of the 121st, 15th, 14th, and 11th Infantry Regiments. Isolating the whereabouts of these regiments, Volckmann divided North Luzon into five military "districts":

District 1—66th Infantry   District 2—121st Infantry
District 3—15th Infantry   District 4—11th Infantry
District 5—14th Infantry

The 66th Infantry was a composite unit that Volckmann created especially for the occasion. It consisted of three battalions that had previously belonged to other regiments prior to the invasion. During the retreat, 1st Battalion, 43rd Infantry (Philippine Scouts), 2nd Battalion, 11th Infantry (Philippine Army), and 3rd Battalion, 12th Infantry (Philippine Army) were separated from their parent units along the western coast of Luzon. Now within Volckmann's command, he organized the lost battalions into one regiment. Adding together the numerical designations of their former regiments (43, 11, and 12 for a total of 66) he designated them as the 66th Infantry.

Establishing his General Headquarters (GHQ) at the camp in Haliap, Volckmann organized these districts under one command: *The United States Armed Forces in the Philippines—North Luzon* (USAFIP-NL). Blackburn sent copies of the Table of Organization to all of Volckmann's subordinate commanders. One commander would be assigned to each district who would then assume control of all units and personnel operating within that district.

By the dawn of 1944, it had become clear that the North Luzon partisans had survived the worst of their growing pains. They were no longer a fragmented hodgepodge of displaced USAFFE personnel and angry natives. "A guerrilla force now existed not just on paper, but in squads, companies, and in some sections, battalions. Five camps had been established in Ifugao. Communications had been constantly maintained with guerrillas in other areas like Benguet and Nueva Vizcaya."

February 14. Happy Birthday, Ann. I hope your feminine intuition makes you feel that I'm still alive.

March 1. This area has been quiet for the past two weeks, according to the reports I've received. All Jap patrols have returned to their garrisons except one and they have learned nothing except how hard it is to climb mountains.

I am reorganizing. Bunnol is now commanding A Company, Balanban is commanding B Company. Balanban is still the men's favorite but Bunnol gets results quicker. I can see that as our organization grows I will have to delegate more and more authority.

Radio news of February 17 included in messages from Benguet (and always two weeks behind the event) reports the capture of the Marshall Islands. I figure that it will take me about two months to complete my reorganization plans and go to work on the enemy.

March 7. Famorca reports from Kiangan that rice is to be controlled in Ifugao. This is a blow. My men live on rice, and we have a hard enough time getting a sufficient supply of it without its being controlled. But I have found that there are always ways and means. Rice control is a problem but if it weren't for these problems life would be dull.

March 8. I went to Camp Two and conferred with the barrio leaders. I instructed them to go out and buy up [the rice] at a price of one peso for four bundles. This is much better than the farmers will get under the confiscation prices that the Japs have set. My prices pleased the barrio leader, who immediately promised me eight cavans [a "cavan" is a Philippine unit of mass roughly equivalent to 60 kg] of rice. This supply will carry our camp to the month of June.

March 12. Lieutenant Bunnol's men recently uncovered more rifles, Garands and two Browning automatics. Our firepower is growing.

After a handful of entries throughout the rest of March and April, Blackburn ended his diary on April 29, 1944. By this time, however, USAFIP-NL had a thorough recordkeeping system and Blackburn's growing responsibility in the organization left him with little time to keep a diary.

Meanwhile, GHQ discovered that Ralph Praeger, the man who

Volckmann had wanted to lead the 11th Infantry (4th District), was dead. He had been captured by the Japanese in March. Thus, to command the scattered remnants of the 11th Infantry in the Cagayan Valley, Volckmann turned to a man whose loyalty and capabilities were beyond reproach—Don Blackburn.

On August 5, 1944, Blackburn received this letter from Volckmann:

1. Organize first the northeastern part of Ifugao.
2. As rapidly as possible, keeping in mind thorough organization, push into eastern Bontoc, then on up into eastern Kalinga.
3. As soon as you are established in eastern Kalinga, push into western Cagayan and eastern Apayao with the idea of locating units and arms in that area.
4. Outside of intelligence work . . . the interior part of Ifugao will be secondary to the above objective.
5. I am sending you an officer who should be a great help to you in the Cagayan valley. He is Lieutenant Tomas Quiocho, who formerly served under Ralph Praeger in Apayao. According to Quiocho, Praeger's guerrillas were broken up by a strong Jap forces operating on information given by spies in Apayao.
6. You are authorized to incorporate any existing units into your command that are now operating in the areas designated above.
7. Your objective and mission is to get into western Cagayan. One precaution, and a principle already given you: do not overlook the organizing of and use of agents in all key barrios and municipalities. They will be your eyes and ears and will aid in keeping your area under control and spies and informers eliminated.

Organizing Bontoc, Kalinga, Cagayan, and Apayao was sure to be a daunting task, but Blackburn accepted it with enthusiasm. Later that month, he began his journey into the Cagayan Valley. He had grown comfortable with the pace of events in Ifugao. With every passing day, more and more volunteers—veterans of the Philippine Army, Philippine Scouts, and native headhunters like Tamicpao and Kamayong—came out of the wilderness to join the guerrillas. Still, within Apayao and the Cagayan Valley, there were many questions that Blackburn needed to have answered. Most notably: What had happened to Ralph Praeger? Blackburn's new operational area included part of the 5th District, which already belonged to Major Romulo Manriquez. Yet, Manriquez's reports always indicated a lack of progress with the guerrilla movement there. Now that Blackburn was taking over part of Manriquez's region, he wanted to find out why guerrilla operations were taking so long to gain traction there. The reason, as Blackburn would soon discover, was quite disturbing.

Blackburn departed Ifugao with his normal entourage—Bruno, Emilio, Basilio Tayaban, and Emiliano Dulnuan. This time, however, they were accompanied by six Ifguao bodyguards armed with Bolo knives and Garand rifles. His first stop was the barrio of Hapao, to inspect Alfredo Bunnol's new camp. Bunnol had since built his company into an entire battalion (~250 men) and constructed a camp made of cogon grass barracks.

Satisfied with the state of Bunnol's camp, Blackburn went on to Ubao where he met an elderly man named Mateo Cadelina. Cadelina, using his son Juanito as an interpreter, related to Blackburn the atrocities that had been happening in the Cagayan Valley. A group of savages who called themselves guerrillas were terrorizing the valley. They had looted, plundered, and razed entire villages and had kidnapped many local women. Now Blackburn understood why guerrilla warfare had been so slow to take root in the lower valley: these "guerrillas," whoever they were, had been driving people away from the Phillipine-American cause. Don wondered if Manriquez was aware of the same.

Blackburn asked Cadelina what these "banditos" looked like, to which he replied that they were tall, horse-riding savages who wore long hair down to their waist. In an instant, Blackburn knew that these were the "Longhairs," members of the Ilongot tribe. Many of these tribesmen had been organized into guerrilla units in Manriquez's district.

Determined to get to the bottom of the issue, Blackburn followed Cadelina to his ranch and asked him to assemble as many witnesses as he could to get a full account of the Longhairs' atrocities. Cadelina responded with thirty eyewitnesses, all of whom were residents of Masarat Grande, a local town which had been the Longhairs' latest target. All thirty confirmed the unspeakable brutality of the Longhairs' raids and begged Blackburn to take action.

"Who is the leader of these Longhairs?" Blackburn asked.

"A man named Dumlao," Cadelina replied.

"Where is his headquarters?"

"In a camp a few miles south of the ranch."

"Good, send one of your men to this Dumlao," Don said. Blackburn wanted to confront him in person.

As Cadelina's emissary rode off to the Longhairs' village, and the nervous witnesses scattered to avoid the impending showdown, Blackburn's senses suddenly caught up to him. He had promised action against a group of savages about whom he knew virtually nothing. He had sent a message to their leader who, no doubt, was on his way with several armed comrades. To boot, they were on horseback and Blackburn was on foot. At this point, Don wished he had brought more than just six headhunter bodyguards. But Blackburn knew that if he backed down, the credibility of the guerrilla movement would suffer. "And the inhabitants of the valley, harassed by the bandits and disillusioned by the guerrillas, might turn in disgust to the Japanese for protection." Blackburn couldn't afford either outcome.

While trying to calm his nerves, Blackburn's thoughts were soon interrupted by the sound of thundering hoof beats. Suddenly, fifty men appeared over the horizon, galloping at full speed towards the Cadelina Ranch. Their long hair streamed behind their defiantly scowled faces as they slowed their horses in front of Blackburn and his entourage. Dwarfed by the ruffians on horseback, he could see why these savages had such a fierce reputation. Dumlao was accompanied by his brother, "Dumlao the Younger." The elder Dumlao stayed atop his horse, balefully staring at Blackburn while he let his younger brother do the talking.

Blackburn disguised his apprehension underneath a tough-talking veneer. He told the brothers that they were a disgrace to the USAFFE guerrillas and that no further acts of banditry would be tolerated. He further asked them if they were aware that they were committing these acts in the district of their leader, Major Manriquez.

"And where is this Manriquez?" Dumlao the Younger asked in a snide tone.

Blackburn had no answer. He only wished that Manriquez had resolved these problems months ago instead of sending whiny reports to GHQ. Blackburn told the Longhair brothers that he would remain in the area until they ceased their acts of banditry. However, after a few minutes, Blackburn knew that the conversation with the Dumlaos was going nowehere. With that, he dismissed the Longhairs, who then thundered off over the horizon.

While Blackburn contemplated his next move, he remembered noticing that, during the meeting with Dumlao, none of his Igorot bodyguards had shown the least bit of fear in the presence of the Longhairs. In fact, they seemed genuinely unimpressed by them and even slightly contemptuous. When Blackburn asked his Igorots for their opinion, they told him that the Longhairs were all bark and no bite—"One headhunter from Mountain Province was worth ten lowlanders," they told him. And, if given the chance, they would show Blackburn exactly what they meant.

Blackburn accepted the invitation. He told Cadelina to provide him and his men with some horses. Together, Blackburn and his entourage would ride into the Longhairs village and deliver them an ultimatum: they would either cease their acts of banditry, or the rest of USAFIP-NL would turn against them and "run the Longhairs back across the Magat River into the machine guns of the Japanese." It was a bold move, but the credibility of the guerrilla movement was on the line and Blackburn trusted the word of his Igorot warriors.

As they rode into the Longhair village, Blackburn noticed that it fit nearly every stereotype of a criminal neighborhood. The Longhairs were drinking and fighting along the village's unkempt streets where stood dingy houses made of cogon grass.

"Where is your leader, Dumlao?" Blackburn thundered to a nearby group of Longhairs. Surprised, they quietly pointed to a grass hut down the street. Blackburn then stormed into Dumlao's residence and, with the Igorots at his side, issued Dumlao the following instructions: all kidnapped women would be returned to their homes; all stolen property returned to their rightful owners; and one particular Longhair who was guilty of murdering a farmer's son was to be turned over immediately. "A full report on the activities of the Longhairs was being forwarded immediately to the commander-in-chief of the guerrilla forces [Volckmann] and to Dumlao's superior, Major Manriquez." And if any further acts of terrorism were committed by the Longhairs, they would be forfeited to the Japanese. Considering the atrocities of which the Japanese were capable, Dumlao knew it was better to comply with Blackburn's instructions.

The Dumlao brothers meekly complied and turned over their

comrade wanted for murder. And word of Blackburn's showdown with
the Longhairs travelled fast. Townspeople throughout the region were
thrilled to see their wives and daughters returned, along with their missing property. The one murderous Longhair was then put on trial and
quickly executed. Blackburn had thus earned the respect and admira-
tion of the people throughout Manriquez's district. But Blackburn
couldn't stop thinking about how peculiar this whole situation had
been. These Longhairs were made out to be the most vile and ruthless
criminals of North Luzon. At times, they sounded even worse than
the Japanese. Yet all it took was a small show of force by an American
officer and a handful of Igorot headhunters to tame these so-called
"bandits." Perhaps the Longhairs were nothing more than overgrown
bullies.

Blackburn also wondered why Manriquez hadn't pulled in the
reigns on Dumlao, or if he had even been aware of the criminal activity
happening within his district. Shortly before leaving Masarat Grande,
Blackburn penned a letter to Manriquez outlining the charges against
the Longhairs and requested a meeting with him to further discuss the
matter.

The next stop on Blackburn's reorganization tour was Tuao. He established a temporary headquarters there and was soon joined by two
other men: Tomas Quiochco, the Philippine Army lieutenant whom
Volckmann had mentioned in his letter from August 5, and Barris, a
former taxi driver. Barris had run afoul of the Japanese during the early
days of the Occupation. One morning, Barris had driven the Japanese
"puppet president," Jose P. Laurel, to a local golf club in Manila. Minutes after leaving Barris' cab, Laurel was shot and wounded in a brutal
assassination attempt. Thinking that the cab driver had been an acces-
sory to the crime, the Kempai Tai arrested him and locked him away at
Fort Santiago. Although Barris had nothing to do with the assassination
plot, the Japanese did not believe him. He was later released and
acquitted of all charges, but his tenure at Fort Santiago was marked by
severe torture and savage beatings. At one point, the Japanese had
forced him to drink diluted sulfuric acid to obtain a confession—a
stomach pump narrowly saved his life. A third new arrival was a
woman, Socorro Viloria, a former nun who had forsaken her vows and
pledged her service as a spy for the guerrillas.

In a letter dated October 5, 1944, Blackburn conveyed the following updates to Volckmann:

1. I have written Manriquez of my findings in his District. I hope he does not resent my frankness.
2. I have contacted a doctor who wants to join up, Calbes Diego of Masarat Grande. I have commissioned him a First Lieutenant and given him the immediate mission of buying up all the medical supplies he can find in Masarat Grande.
3. Joaquin Dunuan [a Philippine Army captain who had joined the guerrillas in August] are reporting progress to the north [organizing guerrilla companies in said area]. Dunuan has organized three companies in his new sector. He reports that the mayor of Pinukpuk is pro-Jap and has sent him an ultimatum. Swick [who recently escaped from his Japanese prison camp] is in or near the town of Tuao. I sent Lieutenant Quiocho north to Swick. Dunuan and Swick are operating in bad malaria and blackwater fever country and I can use any amount of quinine you can spare.
4. Recruits are coming in all the time. One of the recent ones, Lieutenant Agneo, claims to have been in touch with one of Robert Arnold's guerrillas. I sent one of my new agents, Miss Socorro Viloria, into the area where Arnold was reported to be, and she confirmed Lieutenant Agneo's story. So I am sending Agneo into the same area with a letter from me that may convince Arnold that our attempts to bring him in are not a trap.
5. I have enclosed letters for the United States. I have sealed one to Miss Ann Smith. I can assure your headquarters that nothing of importance from a military or Japanese viewpoint is included. But if same must be censored then go to it.

A few days later, Robert Arnold finally showed up. Arnold was another guerrilla who had been hit particularly hard by the Japanese's anti-guerrilla campaign. When he stumbled into Blackburn's camp, he was dreadfully sick and emaciated from his toils in the Philippine wilderness. At this point, Arnold had suffered some very "disillusioning experiences with ineffectual leaders" in the early days of the guerrilla movement. However, when Blackburn showed him the progress that USAFIP-NL had made in just one short year, Arnold shook off his cynicism and eventually commanded one of Volckmann's guerrilla regiments.

Meanwhile, a young Navy Pilot—Lieutenant Jack Bowen—had crashlanded in the Cagayan Valley and had been recovered by the local natives. He soon found his way into a guerrilla camp where he brought some exciting news from the outside world: the Allied invasion of the Philippines was to begin on October 20, 1944.

Finally, towards the end of October, Manriquez appeared at Masarat Grande to see if the accusations against the Longhairs were true. To show Manriquez the gravity of the situation, Blackburn convened a court at Masarat Grande where the victims could confront the Dumlaos and make a public record of their grievances. With Blackburn and Manriquez presiding, the court took session at the Cadelina Ranch. In the opening testimony, an elderly man recounted the atrocities that the Longhairs had committed, at which point, Dumlao the Younger stood up and grabbed the witness, shouting "You're a liar! And if you know what's good for you, you'll tell the truth!"

Don Blackburn, already fed up with the Dumlaos' behavior, grabbed the younger brother and, with a violent shove, sent the heckling bandit crashing to the floor. "Get over there, stay over there, and keep your God-damn mouth shut!" Blackburn bellowed. Dumlao the Younger, shaken by his comeuppance, meekly obeyed and the witnesses continued their damning testimony against the Longhairs. By the end of the trial, Manriquez was convinced of the truth and issued a firm warning to the elder Dumlao. The Longhair chieftain was allowed to keep his command, but if there were any more acts of banditry, the Longhairs would be treated as enemies.

On November 4, 1944, Blackburn departed for Tuao. He turned the Ubao camp into a message center and left Juanito Cadelina, whom Blackburn had recently inducted, in charge of it. After two days on the trail, Blackburn and company arrived in Tuao to some disheartening news. The Japanese, anxious to recapture Herb Swick, learned that he had been hiding in Tuao and subsequently raided the village. Fortunately, Swick got out just ahead of the raid and had purportedly moved to the nearby village of Pinukpuk.

As Blackburn crossed the Chico River en route to Pinukpuk, he turned to one of his native guides and asked how far it was to the village. "Very near," they answered. But Don knew that the natives had a very different concept of distance. "Very near" could mean a few hours or even a few days. Attempting to get a more accurate answer, he pointed to the sun and said, "The sun is there. Where will be it when we arrive?" The natives then pointed to a spot just above the horizon, and Blackburn continued down the trail, thinking that the journey would be over by nightfall. But as the sun went down over the horizon, they were still hiking at full gait. Once again, he had been fooled by the Filipinos' over-optimistic sense of distance. Luckily, through the darkness of the trail, the group found a small lean-to which they hurriedly squeezed into and started a small campfire.

At daybreak the group lit out for Pinukpuk and arrived in the barrio after only an hour. Unfortunately, the natives said that Swick had moved yet again to Ripang, only a few miles to the northwest. Continuing their hike, they reached the outskirts of Ripang where Herb Swick and his lieutenant were waiting for them. Greeting each other with a hug and a good-spirited slap on the back, Swick and Blackburn jaunted into Ripang, where a crowd of cheering townspeople had prepared a feast just for them. After the feast, however, Blackburn wanted to know what had happened in Tuao.

Ruefully, Swick admitted that he had let his guard down. As it happened, the people of Tuao were decidedly pro-American and decided to show their appreciation by throwing a lavish party for Swick and his men. However, Swick enjoyed the leisurely affair to the detriment of his security. For not until the last minute did he catch wind of the Japanese patrol that was on its way to the village. Without a moment to lose, Swick, his top sergeant, and ten of his men took to their heels and settled into a small barrio about five miles north of Tuao. Meanwhile, a torrential rainstorm outside grew into a fierce typhoon. His men slept peacefully, but Swick himself couldn't sleep a wink. His men were confident that the Japanese wouldn't chase them through the storm, but Swick wasn't so sure. Taking solace in the typhoon was exactly what the Japanese would have wanted them to do. Listening to his gut, Swick ordered his men to pack up and find a new hiding place.

"Are you out of your mind, sir? The Japs won't come after us in a typhoon."

"That's just when those bastards *will* come after us," Swick said.

"I was captured once and I don't intend to be captured again. Let's get the hell out of here."

But Swick's men wouldn't budge. They were convinced that the Japanese wouldn't brave the typhoon. Swick didn't try to force their compliance but left, saying, "Well, you guys are stupid if you stay." With that, Swick and his sergeant, along with two of his men, stumbled their way through the typhoon.

A few hours later, however, Swick's prophecy came true. The Japanese patrol had indeed left Tuao and, unshaken by the typhoon, marched across the jungle. Fast asleep in their "evacuation hut," Swick's men were surrounded, captured, and bayoneted to death by the Japanese.

At Ripang, Swick had inducted another guerrilla who had served under Ralph Praeger, a young man named Felipe. Felipe had distinguished himself by tracking down those who had betrayed Ralph Praeger to the Japanese. With a platoon of guerrillas at his back, Felipe rounded up all the Japanese sympathizers in Ripang. Searching through their records, he found a letter written by the Mayor of Ripang listing the names of those who had contributed to Praeger's capture. He then worked his way down the list until, one by one, the people who had betrayed Ralph Praeger were dead.

After getting his updates from Swick, Blackburn decided to relocate his headquarters to Kabugao, the capital of the Apayao sub-province. He knew that he would probably have to move his headquarters again soon, but Kabugao at least gave him a good platform to keep an eye on enemy activity and maintain a reasonable command and control of his growing battalions. Furthermore, Kabugao was a three-day hike from the nearest Japanese garrison.

Settling into his new headquarters, Blackburn outlined his strategy for the Cagayan Valley. The Japanese controlled the entire valley, from Aparri in the north to Enrile in the south. To secure the Cagayan Valley, "Blackburn's Headhunters" would have to clear the Japanese from the towns of Tuao, Solana, Enrile, Tuguegarao, and Aparri. Throughout the planning phase, Blackburn knew that Tuguegarao and Aparri would be his priority targets. Aparri, a seaport town on the northern shore of Luzon, sat at the mouth of the Cagayan River. It was also the first stop for Japanese naval convoys sending reinforcements and materiel to North Luzon. Tuguegarao stood at the crossroads of the eastern provinces in North Luzon. Plus, the Japanese garrison at Tuguegarao was huge and could easily send or receive reinforcements from the other garrisons in Mountain Province.

However, Blackburn would have to start small. Before taking on the Japanese at Aparri or Tuguegarao, he would have to clear the enemy's "fifth column" from Solana. According to Herb Swick, Solana was a hotbed of enemy spies. But the town's most disgusting character was the spy ringleader, Avena. Before the war, Avena had been a successful merchandiser at a department store in Manila. As the Japanese closed in on city, he had taken advantage of the ensuing chaos and looted from various retailers. After the Fall of Bataan, he made a name for himself on the Philippine black market, but avoided the enmity of the Japanese by sharing some of his profits with the Kempai Tai.

He had since moved his black market operations to Solana and maintained a good rapport with the Japanese by financing one of the largest spy rings in North Luzon. Swick attributed his recent troubles in Tuao to Avena's spy network. Capturing Solana would break up the spy ring and allow the guerrillas to interdict the Japanese mercantile operations there. As it turned out, the town's warehouses had been bought by two Japanese businessmen named Toyaminka and Gunmai. Gunmai and his associates had bought up all the rice in the valley for pennies on the dollar. In return, Gunmai issued the farmers a voucher with which they could buy various dry goods from Toyaminka's gang.

Collectively, the Japanese-owned warehouses carried enough rice to feed the regiment for six months. The Toyaminka dry goods, if captured by the guerrillas, could easily be bartered and perhaps take some of the pressure off Blackburn's IOU recordkeeping. Don therefore decided to probe Solana with a late-night raid. In doing so, he hoped to test the town's defenses, strike fear into the town's spy ring, and give the guerrillas a much-needed boost to their confidence after their hasty retreat from Tuao. For the initial raid, he selected Company A from Herb Swick's battalion. The guerrillas would send two platoons to capture Avena while the other two platoons—on the other side of town—would break into the Japanese warehouses and carry out as much as they could fit on their oxcarts.

On the night of the raid, Company A entered Solana uncontested. The oxcarts were placed precipitously outside the warehouses, waiting for their armed escorts to punch through the doors and begin loading the Japanese goods. All seemed to be going well until the guerrillas reached Avena's house.

It turned out that Avena had rigged an early warning system to his house in the event that any "banditos" paid him an unexpected visit. When he awoke to the sound of approaching guerrillas, Avena alerted his accomplices who then poured into the streets with their guns blazing. Shaken by the sudden gunfire, the guerrillas forced their way into Avena's home, but in the ensuing melee the traitorous merchant escaped. Meanwhile, at the other end of town, the guerrillas at the warehouse heard the oncoming gunfire and fled the scene—abandoning the oxcarts where they stood. With the operation falling apart, Company A aborted the mission and took to their heels. They made it out of town relatively unscathed, but the worst was yet to come. Avena had alerted the Japanese commander, who responded by reopening the garrison in Solana and increasing patrols along the Cagayan Valley.

Although the raid on Solana was a disappointment, Blackburn refused to let it slow him down. He redoubled his efforts in the training and marksmanship program and reorganized the civilian auxiliary. Accordingly, he split the auxiliary into two gender-based groups: the Bolomen and the Women's Auxiliary Service (WAS). Bolomen, so named for the primitive bolo knives they carried, were barrio-dwellers or headhunting natives who acted as guards, spies, and general laborers. The WAS performed all domestic and hospitality services for the guerrillas—cooking, cleaning, sewing, and tending to sick soldiers.

And then there was the issue of firearms. The Philippine Scouts still had their Garands and the Philippine Army soldiers still had their unreliable Enfields. Many of the barrio residents carried pistols and rifles of various calibers, while the headhunters preferred their bolo knives. Still, Blackburn knew the Japanese had him outgunned. And he needed more than just a ragtag arsenal of semi-automatic weapons to drive them from the Cagayan Valley.

Fortunately, Don received an encouraging note from Russ Volckmann. While Don had been organizing his regiment in the Cagayan Valley, Russ had been trading messages with MacArthur's HQ in Australia. This radio traffic resulted in a submarine, the *USS Gar*, being dispatched to North Luzon with twenty tons of supplies, including arms, ammunition, and medicine. Volckmann's communiqué also stated that "Blackburn's Headhunters" were slated to receive a portion of it. When the submarine finally landed in October 1944, Volckmann sent Blackburn several crates of dynamite, Thompson machine guns, rifles, bazookas, grenades, and grenade launchers. There was also a generous supply of medicine for Blackburn's men who had come down with malaria and blackwater fever. Blackburn generously divided the medicine and weapons amongst his men.

Meanwhile, twelve of Blackburn's soldiers delivered a prisoner to the Kabugao headquarters. His name was Hillary P. Clapp, the Governor of Bontoc sub-province. He was a Filipino who had taken a Christian name upon his conversion to the Anglican Faith. As Governor, however, Clapp had fallen at the feet of the Japanese. He actively collaborated with the enemy during the anti-guerrilla campaign of 1942–43 and, through Felipe's fact-finding mission, was found to be an accomplice in Ralph Praeger's execution. Clapp himself was later executed by Blackburn's men.

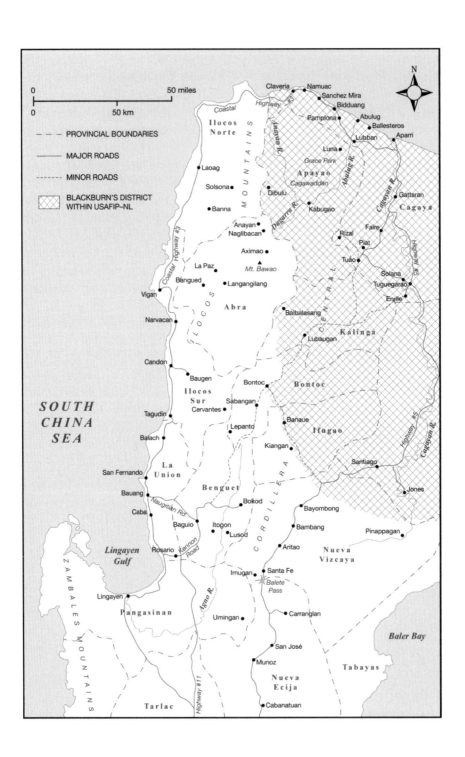

N

0   50 miles
0   50 km

‒ ‒ ‒ PROVINCIAL BOUNDARIES
───── MAJOR ROADS
─ ─ ─ MINOR ROADS
⊠ BLACKBURN'S DISTRICT
    WITHIN USAFIP–NL

Coastal Highway #3

Ilocos Norte

MOUNTAINS

Agurra R.

Claveria   Namuac
              Sanchez Mira
              Bidduang
Pamplona   Abulug
                   Ballesteros
         Lubban   Aparri
    Luna
    Grace Park
Apayao   *Cagayan R.*
Cagawaddan
Dibulu
              Gattaran
  Kabugao   **Cagaya**

Laoag
Solsona

Banna

Anayan
Naglibacan
                Rizal
  Aximao   Piat
             Faire
La Paz   ▲ *Mt. Bawao*   Tuao
Bangued   *Langangilang*
                         Solana
Vigan   Tuguegarao
                         Enrile

Ilocos   **Abra**
              Balbalasang

Narvacan

                Kalinga
            Lubaugan
Candon

Baugen
        Bontoc
Ilocos   **Bontoc**
Sur   Sabangan
Tagudin   Cervantes
          Lepanto   Banaue
Balach   **Ifugao**
            Kiangan

                Santiago
San Fernando
                        Jones
Bauang
        Naugrian Rd **Benguet**
Caba   Bokod
                            Bayombong
   Baguio   Itogon   Bambang
            Lusod   Pinappagan
Kennon Road   Aritao
Rosario   **Nueva**
                 Vizcaya
Lingayen
Gulf   Imugan   Santa Fe
                     Balete Pass
Lingayen
        Agno R.
Pangasinan   Umingan   Carranglan

                                  Baler Bay

            San José
         Munoz   **Tabayas**
ZAMBALES MOUNTAINS
         Nueva
         Ecija
Tarlac Highway #11   Cabanatuan

SOUTH CHINA SEA

CORDILLERA

CENTRAL

Highway #5   *Cagayan R.*

Dagura R.
Abulug R.

CHAPTER 8

COMBAT OPERATIONS

While recalibrating his forces in the wake of the Solana Raid, Blackburn turned his attention north to the coastal towns of Lubban, Claveria, and Ballesteros. Clearing the enemy from these towns meant clearing them from the entire northern coast west of the Cagayan River. Because these towns couldn't easily be reinforced by the Japanese, Blackburn decided to conduct his sweep-and-clear mission with only two companies, F and H, and selected Herb Swick to lead the attack.

Travelling west along Highway 3, Swick began his coastal campaign at Claveria. Within minutes, his two companies destroyed the Japanese garrison and saved the town's sawmill before the Japanese had a chance to burn it. Deciding to give his men a day's rest before pushing on to Lubban, Swick received an unexpected surprise from the sea. Suddenly, two Japanese naval vessels appeared over the horizon: a troop carrier and a cargo ship. The two ships barreled through the surf towards the Claveria docks, completely unaware that the guerrillas were waiting for them. Swick, marveling at the sight, waited for the enemy to come ashore. Fifty Japanese soldiers disembarked from the watercraft when Swick gave the order to open fire.

When the smoke cleared, forty-eight Japanese were dead and the remaining two, a lieutenant and a medic, were taken prisoner. From the enemy's vessels, the guerrillas recovered food, medicine, a handful of two-way radios, two automatic rifles, and an 81mm mortar. Mean-

111

while, the two shell-shocked enemy captives translated the medicine labels and showed the guerrillas how to load and use the Japanese guns.

With his latest windfall, Swick hastened his departure to Lubban. The following night, his two companies crossed the Abulang River and took the Japanese garrison with surprisingly little resistance. During the attack, the Japanese realized that they couldn't hold their position with the guerrillas flanking them from both sides, and fled to their sister garrison at Ballesteros. Although the Japanese decided to make a stand at Ballesteros, it was of little use—Swick's men overran the garrison and counted 93 dead Japanese by the end of the engagement. Swick's march on the northern coast put him only five miles west of Aparri. Blackburn, however, decided to hold off on the siege of Aparri until he could clear Tuao.

Establishing his new headquarters in Tuao, Blackburn gave himself the base he needed to attack Solana. Tuao was only about 10 miles west of Solana and both were frequented by Japanese patrols. But just across the river lay the guerrillas' ultimate prize, Tuguegarao. It was the second largest city in North Luzon (behind Baguio) and the Japanese had made it their regional headquarters for the Cagayan Valley. It was obviously an important base as the Japanese had built two airfields around it and fortified the city with tanks and artillery.

On the morning of January 24, 1945, Blackburn took his entourage—Bruno, Emilio, and Barris—into Tuao to rendezvous with Herb Swick, who was returning from his coastal campaign up north. The news of their arrival must have sent a shockwave through the valley because Blackburn and Swick were soon overrun by more volunteers (most of them former Philippine Army and Scouts) than they could count.

The new crop of volunteers also allowed Blackburn to fill the ranks of his regimental staff. He had heretofore been his own operations officer, intelligence officer, and supply officer. Now, he had found the right men for each of these jobs. The Intelligence Section (S-2) was the one he needed to reorganize the most. Blackburn had done a decent job assembling intelligence reports from spies like Socorro Viloria and his friends in the barrio, but critical details remained sketchy. Volckmann sent Blackburn a sum of 45,000 pesos to hire new agents just as Don found the right man for his intelligence work: Lieutenant Mariano Manawis, Philippine Army. Manawis had been captured during the retreat to Bataan and, after a short stint inside a Japanese prison camp, he was released and allowed to return to his family in Tuao. Manawis was a very bright and forward-thinking man who revitalized the intelligence operations for the 11th Infantry. "With the intelligence fund, Manawis bought the services of people in the river towns like Solana and Enrile and in the city of Tuguegarao itself. In his office at the guerrilla headquarters in Tuao, Manawis constructed an elaborate mosaic on which the Cagayan Valley was divided into areas that varied in size with their strategic importance."

For the position of Regimental Executive Officer (XO), Blackburn selected Major Rafael Pargas. A graduate of the US Naval Academy, Pargas transferred from the Navy to the Philippine Army upon his return from the United States. Captain William Burke became Black-

Don Blackburn with comrades (from left to right), Rafael Pargas, Mrs. Lita Pargas, and Herb Swick, 1945. The Donald D. Blackburn Collection

burn's Supply Officer (S-4). Burke was a Philippine *mestizo*—born to an American father and a Filipina mother—and an extremely capable logistician. Another arrival in Tuao was Captain Deogracias Caballero, who signed on as Blackburn's Regimental Operations Officer (S-3). Another new arrival was Major Eugenio Balao, who became the 11th Infantry's Inspector General.

Meanwhile, Soccorro Viloria kept herself busy sketching enemy fortifications and sabotaging the same whenever the opportunity arose. Her weapon of choice was a small device known as an "incendiary pencil." A crate of these pencils had arrived in one of the resupply submarines, and the guerrillas quickly put them to good use. The device itself was a small vial of acid encased in a metal shield which separated the vial from an explosive charge. If the vial was broken, the acid would bleed through the metal shield and activate the charge. This gave the saboteur just enough time to flee the scene before the target would go up in flames. Viloria dropped several of these pencils into Japanese fuel depots along the Cagayan River.

By mid-February 1945, Blackburn's regiment was operating at full-strength. The 1st Battalion, under Captain Alfredo Bunnol was fighting in Buntoc and Ifugao. 2nd Battalion, under Herb Swick, had split its companies: two remained in the north outside of Aparri while the other two staged a few miles north of Tuguegarao. Meanwhile, 3rd Battalion was clearing the enemy from Kalinga.

Joaquin Dunuan, the commander of 3rd Battalion, had been sending reconnaissance patrols into Lubuagan where he had spotted the Japanese building a new arms depot. Realizing that his battalion didn't have the resources to take the depot by force, Dunuan bided his time. The enemy depot was heavily manned but Dunuan knew that the Japanese couldn't provide reinforcements for it—guerrilla activity elsewhere in the Cagayan Valley had tied up all available troops. Thus, every time a Japanese patrol left the depot, Dunuan would set an ambush for them. Eventually, the Japanese depot lost so many of its men to the ambushes that they could no longer repel an assault on the installation. When Dunuan finally gave the order to attack, the Japanese defenders were easily overrun. At the end of his epic raid on the depot, every Japanese soldier had been killed and Dunuan had enough rifles and machine guns for the entire battalion.

As news of Dunuan's victory reached 11th Infantry headquarters,

Blackburn was finalizing his plan for a second raid on Solana. He had selected Company E from Herb Swick's battalion and tapped Lieutenant Tomas Quiocho to lead the mission. Quiocho's men were eager to bring the fight to the Japanese, but Blackburn worried that they might be too green and their firepower too weak. Blackburn's fears, however, were quickly dispelled. Although the Japanese initially pushed Quiocho's men to the edge of the river, the company quickly regrouped. Quiocho then left half of his men on the river banks and took the other half around the far side of the bank to attack the Japanese from the rear. Frightened by the sudden crossfire, the enemy retreated back to Solana. The Japanese attacked again the following morning and Quiocho, using the same maneuver, outflanked the enemy and sent them retreating to Solana yet again. At nightfall, Quiocho split up his company to make one frontal and two flank attacks on the Solana garrison. "By this time, the Japanese must have decided that they were being assaulted by a whole battalion of guerrillas; they used the only remaining exit and crossed the Cagayan by boat. The Japanese garrison at Enrile took their cue from this exodus and also withdrew across the river."

With the capture of Solana, the guerrillas also nabbed Avena, the traitorous merchant. He was taken prisoner and sentenced to hard labor in one of the guerrilla camps. Securing the town also broke up the dreaded spy ring and gave the guerrillas unlimited access to the Gunmai and Toyaminka warehouses. But there was still work to be done. Blackburn's men had driven the Japanese from the west banks of the Cagayan, but he knew it wouldn't be long before the enemy tried to retake it. Don therefore placed two of his battalions along the river, stretching from Enrile to the northern coast of Luzon. Bolomen would patrol the river banks while the combat companies stood ready at mobile defense bases that would allow them to reinforce any point on the river where the Japanese might attack.

Blackburn's hunches proved correct; one week after the enemy's exodus from Solana and Enrile, they tried to take back their garrisons. After prepping both towns with mortar and machine-gun fire, the Japanese attempted a river crossing a few miles north of Solana. However, a Bolomen patrol quickly spotted the enemy watercraft and alerted a nearby company from Dunuan's battalion. With the firearms they had taken from Japanese depot at Lubuagan, Dunuan's company destroyed the enemy flotilla. Those who tried to escape were quickly manhandled and drowned by the pursuing guerrillas. Not one Japanese soldier made it back to the east bank. These operations continued for the next several weeks: the Japanese would attempt to cross the river, barely making it to the other side before their landing party was either shot or drowned by the carefully concealed Igorots. By the time the Japanese gave up trying to cross the river, they had lost over 3,000 soldiers.

But as the Japanese gave up on their river-crossing operations, Dunuan's men initiated their own. One night, a company from 3rd Battalion floated across the river and captured a six-vehicle convoy moving along Highway 5. The convoy also included a bulldozer, which, along with the other five vehicles, the Igorots brought back to Regimental Headquarters. The bulldozer was a welcomed addition and Blackburn gave it to his engineer company so they could start on an airfield. However, the Igorots' reception at the headquarters was dampened by what they carried with them. Besides delivering the bulldozer and the trucks, the Igorots proudly displayed the severed heads of every Japanese soldier who had been on the convoy. Blackburn didn't know whether to be proud or appalled by the sight. Trying not to wince or gag, Blackburn simply thanked the Igorots for their bravery and dedication.

With the bulldozer on hand, the 11th Infantry engineers cleared a landing strip at Tuao. And the first plane to make its landing there carried Russ Volckmann, making his first visit to Blackburn since the latter's relocation to the western coast of Luzon. As always, Volckmann and Blackburn had much to talk about. The previous month (January 1945), Volckmann had secured the Lingayen Beach in advance of the Allied landings there. When the Allied task force, which included the US Sixth Army, finally arrived at Lingayen, Volckmann met with General MacArthur to discuss the enemy situation in North Luzon. During the meeting, MacArthur promoted Volckmann to full Colonel and authorized a promotion to Lieutenant Colonel for Blackburn.

After their hearty rounds of handshakes and backslaps, Blackburn took Volckmann to inspect the Tuao headquarters as well as the camps at Solana and Enrile. Volckmann, satisfied with the state of Blackburn's camps, departed the Tuao airfield saying that he would send another liaison plane the following week to take Don back to GHQ at Darigayos. When the plane picked him up as promised, Blackburn recalled that it was the first time in nearly four years that he had a chance to relax. For one moment, he no longer had to worry about the Japanese, enemy informers, the intrigue, or the politicking. Now, he was on his way back from behind enemy lines, to a place where the American military called the shots.

As his plane made its final descent into Darigayos, Don noticed the vast naval armada lingering off the shore—and this time it was American. From the airstrip at Darigayos, Volckmann arranged a car to take Blackburn to a local clubhouse which had become the de-facto American Officer's Club. Coincidentally, Blackburn ran into one of his old classmates from the University of Florida, Captain Johnny Allison, who was now an Army Air Force pilot. Allison took Blackburn up in a small liaison plane to survey the progress of the American beachheads. During the flight, they passed over Bauang and the Nagulian Road where, three and a half years earlier, Blackburn and his Ilocanos had fled from the Japanese invasion. Suddenly, the names and the faces of his comrades came back to him: Charlie Youngblood, Harry Kuykendall, Shelby Newman, Eddie Bliss, George Williams, Martin Moses, and Arthur Noble—all of whom were dead now. Choking back the tears over his lost comrades, Blackburn returned to Darigayos later that evening, ready to take on the next chapter in his war against the Japanese.

Throughout March 1945, the 11th Infantry continued to enlist more recruits and expand its operations. Including the spies and Bolomen, "Blackburn's Headhunters" numbered about 5,000. By this time, the guerrillas and pro-American spies operated so efficiently within the Cagayan Valley that the Japanese's informers decided to quit the business. Meanwhile, the mayors and barrio leaders who had previously ridden the fence were now jumping to the American side. The airstrip at Tuao, previously only wide enough to accommodate liaison planes and tactical fighters, had been so improved and expanded that "now as many fifteen C-47s were parked on the field at one time, and the revetments protected the parked planes from any enemy attacks emanating from Tuguegarao." Meanwhile, Manawis turned his mobile strategy map into a target map for the Army Air Force. Manawis would radio the locations of the Japanese supply and fuel depots to a nearby airbase in the Lingayen Gulf. A squadron of P-38s would then take flight over the mountains and rain fire on the targets designated by Blackburn's S-2.

*Blackburn and his Headquarters Staff outside of their guerrilla
headquarters in Tuao, Cagayan.* The Donald D. Blackburn Collection

But as Don continued to expand his operations, Volckmann hit him
with a rather inconvenient redistribution of forces. Herb Swick's 2nd
Battalion was to be transferred, temporarily, to the 3rd District. As a
replacement for Swick's battalion, Volckmann sent Blackburn one of
Romulo Manriquez's units from the 14th Infantry—it was the 1st
Battalion, Dumlao's Longhairs. Needless to say, Blackburn wasn't
thrilled by the reassignment. He hadn't forgotten about the trouble the
Longhairs had caused him and he had no guarantees that they wouldn't
revert to their previous behavior. Nonetheless, Blackburn accepted his
orders and assigned the Longhairs to the lower Valley near Enrile and
Solana.

The Sixth Army offensive in the Cagayan Valley began with the insertion of Task Force Baker and its rendezvous with Blackburn's guerrillas
at Ballesteros. Task Force Baker was a US Army force containing
elements of the 6th Ranger Battalion, 127th Infantry, 510th Engineers,
694th Field Artillery, and other logistical support units. Prior to the
rendezvous, Blackburn received word that Baker's advance would be

slowed due to the numerous river crossings they anticipated to make. Attempting to accelerate the rendezvous, Blackburn ordered his guerrilla engineers to empty their captured sawmill at Claveria and build bridges along the path of Baker's advance. The wood from the sawmill was Philippine mahogany, which Blackburn knew to be remarkably strong, but his engineers lacked sophisticated tools. In fact, all they had were simple machines: hand tools, sledgehammers, and makeshift construction equipment. The engineers finished the bridge in good time, and although it looked sturdy, Don wondered if it would accommodate Baker's tonnage.

That June, Baker rendezvoused with Blackburn at the first guerrilla-made bridge along their route. The commander of Baker's engineer detachment inspected the bridge and seemed genuinely impressed by its design and construction. He turned to Blackburn and asked, "What is this made of, mahogany?"

"Yes," Blackburn replied. "Think it'll hold thirty-five tons?"

"My God, that bridge will hold seventy-five tons!" the engineer captain answered. With the fear of the bridge's suitability behind him, Blackburn briefed the Task Force Commander, Major Robert Connolly, on the plan to lay siege to Aparri.

Even though they were operating in enemy territory, the guerrillas controlled the west side of the Cagayan River, which arguably had better terrain and more maneuver space than the Japanese had on the eastern side. The only two obstacles to capturing Aparri were a lone garrison at Babuyan and the intersection of Highway 5 and the Gonzaga Road. The Babuyan garrison stood atop a hill surrounded by open terrain that provided no cover to a potential attacker. From atop its revetments, the Japanese could train their guns on the advancing guerrillas before they even got close to the garrison walls. The Highway 5 intersection, according to Miss Viloria, was the main thoroughfare by which the Japanese were sending reinforcements south from Aparri to halt the Americans' northward advance. If the highway were destroyed at the intersection of the Gonzaga Road, all southbound reinforcements would be trapped.

Blackburn knew, however, that he could mitigate these obstacles with artillery fire. It would eliminate most of the resistance and make the drive to Aparri easier for the Baker-Headhunter group. Emplacing his forces for the assault on Babuyan, Blackburn began the attack with a barrage of shells. Major Connolly then gave his men the order to charge. Meanwhile, Lieutenant Quiocho's men swept over the hill and into the enemy's defenses. Connolly's men met Quiocho's at the top of the Babuyan hill where, together, they stormed the enemy garrison and quickly pacified it. Both Task Force Baker and the guerrillas were surprised that enemy resistance hadn't been stronger. However, in the course of rounding up prisoners and counting the dead, Blackburn's men discovered that most of the Babuyan defenders had slipped out the night before and retreated to Aparri.

The next day, Blackburn's artillery began to soften up the Highway 5 road junction and, feeling that Connolly and Quiocho had the situation well in hand, he decided to return to Headquarters to begin planning the siege of Tuguegarao. For the main body of the attack, Blackburn had two battalions at his disposal: his organic 3rd Battalion and Dumlao's bandit battalion. On June 17, 1945 Blackburn issued the operations order for the capture of Tuguegarao. It was to be a two-pronged attack: 3rd Battalion (Joaquin Dunuan's men) would attack the city from the southwest while Dumlao's would attack directly from

A 1940 postcard depicting the rice terraces of Ifugao. This is a representative sample of the rough terrain upon which Blackburn operated during his guerrilla days.
The Donald D. Blackburn Collection

the west, crossing the Cagayan River at Solana. A squadron of P-38s would provide close air support, and the whole operation was set to begin on June 20.

The siege of Tuguegarao started on a high note with the P-38s bombing and strafing the Japanese defenses. While the American planes conducted their spectacular airstrike, Dumlao and Dunuan moved their battalions into position. At first, Dumlao met only token resistance as his men stormed across the airfield north of the city. The 3rd Battalion ran into a more heavily mounted resistance, but by noon they had forced themselves into the city proper. All seemed well as the two battalions pushed farther into the city, but in the pre-dawn hours of the following morning, Dunuan radioed in that the Japanese were counterattacking with tanks and artillery. Moments later, Dumlao radioed in the same. Realizing that his "siege" was falling apart, Blackburn quickly called for another airstrike. Meanwhile, Dunuan's men were being driven from the city and Dumlao's battalion had lost its foothold in the airfield. Luckily, the airstrike allowed both guerrilla battalions to re-enter the city.

However, later that night, Blackburn received the same bad news he had heard before: enemy counterattack with tanks and artillery. This time, however, it was much worse. Dumlao and his Longhairs were pushed back across the Cagayan River. The 3rd Battalion destroyed two enemy tanks with their bazooka teams, but the enemy armor was so fierce that two of Dunuan's companies took to their heels and retreated into an abandoned prison. Undaunted, the Japanese surrounded the makeshift fortress and continued to fire on the guerrillas until another P-38 strike saved Dunuan's men from a massacre.

Dejected, Blackburn took responsibility for the failure at Tuguegarao. He admitted that he had become too complacent and hadn't dedicated as much time to the project as he should have. He sent a message to Volckmann outlining the defeat. In the letter, Don admitted that he deserved to be relieved of command if Volckmann wished to pursue that option.

"Our losses in this fight were around one hundred and fifty men killed or wounded. I felt wholly to blame for this defeat and should I have been relieved, I would not have complained. I did not plan this attack as thoroughly as I should have; I took too much of a gamble on Dumlao's men, although I always doubted their fighting ability. I was wrong to split my time between Aparri and Tuguegarao. I should have stayed with the fight at Tuguegarao for the situation at Aparri was in good hands. I failed to show the drive I am capable of. To sum up, I made one hell of a mess of the situation and got a lot of killed and wounded. Tuguegarao should have been ours. Our failure to take it wasn't the men's fault; it was the officer's—mine. "

Volckmann nonetheless forgave the mistake and Blackburn did not dwell on it. The following day, he flew up to Aparri to oversee the final assault by Quiocho's men and Task Force Baker. The artillery battery had peppered the town and the enemy's defenses throughout the night. The Ranger company crossed the river to seize the Japanese command posts while Quiocho's guerrillas overran the enemy positions and set up a defense on the Highway 5 intersection. By dawn, the Task Force Baker reconnaissance patrols had combed the outskirts of Aparri, making sure that the enemy had no mechanized assets with which to strike back as they had at Tuguegarao.

Despite this overwhelming victory, however, Blackburn soon received a telegram that essentially took the success away. Volckmann sent word that the 1-511th Airborne Infantry Regiment (11th Airborne Division) was preparing to jump into North Luzon and "capture" Aparri. Blackburn didn't understand; there had to be some mistake. "We've already captured Aparri," he said.

Volckmann explained that this was only a "public relations attack."

By parachuting the 11th Airborne Division into Aparri, the Sixth Army could consolidate all of its forces operating in the Cagayan Valley. Blackburn was a bit disgruntled that his men's (and Baker's) victory was being taken away and the credit given to an airborne battalion that had never set foot in the Cagayan Valley. Still, Blackburn took solace in knowing that his men had opened a clear landing zone for the ever-expanding American reconquest.

On July 1, 1945 authority over North Luzon was transferred from the Sixth Army to the Eighth Army, and with it came a new assignment for Blackburn's men. By this time, his regiment had fought in over 50 battles, large and small, throughout Ifugao, Kalinga, Bontoc, Apayao, and Cagayan. Since their "attachment" to the Sixth Army, most of the 11th Infantry was, as Blackburn said, "engaged in mopping up operations against the Japanese in the Sierra Madre Mountains of the upper Cagayan Valley."

On July 8, Volckmann called Blackburn into his office at the US-AFIP-NL Headquarters. When Blackburn arrived, he saw Volckmann surrounded by several of the US XIV Corps' staff officers. A subordinate corps of the Eighth Army, the XIVth needed Blackburn's men for an important mission. According to the staff officers, "Yamashita's forces on Luzon had been defeated at every turn and were now preparing for a last stand in the very rugged and mountainous terrain west of Highway 4 in the general area of [Banaue, Ifugao]. Another Japanese force estimated from 1,000–2,000, believed to be remnants of ground, air, service, and naval units, organized into Provisional ground force units, was east of Highway 4. This latter force was reported to be concentrating in the vicinity of the town of Mayayao with the intent of making a juncture with Yamashita's force to the west."

Indeed, Yamashita had been on the run since early spring. The so-called "Tiger of Malaya" was losing ground to the advancing Americans and, after his defeat at the Battle of Bessang Pass, he had withdrawn to make his last stand in Ifugao. The force at Mayayao, under Generals Mikami and Marauka, would be especially troublesome. As the US 6th Infantry Division drove north along Highway 11 to attack Yamashita's force at Banaue, the XIV Corps feared that the Mayayao force would attack the Division's rear and disrupt its main supply route. Thus, the 11th Infantry was given the task of destroying the Japanese at Mayayao.

Blackburn knew that his men were up to the task, but his regiment was no longer intact. Herb Swick's battalion was still attached to the 121st Infantry in the 3rd District, "and the 37th Infantry requested the retention of 2nd Battalion," Blackburn said. All he had left were Dumlao's reformed bandits, 3rd Battalion, and the Igorot combat company from his Regimental Headquarters.

"The town of Mayayao," Blackburn said, "was approximately 47 kilometers east of Banaue, and an equal distance west from Masarat Grande in the Cagayan River Valley. Situated at an elevation of about 5,000 feet, the only routes into the town were mountain trails. The rainy season was in full swing, which meant that the only probable means of resupply to a force employed in that area must be by hand carry from Masarat Grande, and/or Banaue, once the 6th Division secured the latter town. Artillery support would be out of the question, and any air support would be dependent on a break in the weather. Evacuation would have to be by hand carry due to the lack of roads and the unavailability of suitable terrain for the construction of an air strip.

"Mayayao was a logical area for the Japanese to concentrate. It was not only remote and difficult to reach, but it was also the largest rice producing area in the mountains remaining accessible to the Japanese, who were in dire need of food. The town was easy to defend, though at an elevation of approximately 5,000 feet; it was situated in a bowl whose surrounding peaks and ridges towered 500–1,000 feet above."

Such were the conditions. "With these facts taken into consideration," Blackburn said, "the following plan was decided upon:

1. The 3rd Battalion, 11th Infantry would depart from Mallig on 13 July, and move to Bunhian via Natonin, avoiding any engagement with the enemy. The Battalion would attack and seize the village, and without delay, would attack the fortified divide east of the village from the rear. It was believed that once Bunhian was captured, the enemy would automatically withdraw from their position on the divide; or if any resistance were offered, it would be meager.
2. The 1st Battalion [Dumlao's Longhairs] would depart from Eden on 13 July, and would advance through the valley and the foothills via Butigui and Dallog to Ubao which was situated at the foot of the divide. Any enemy encountered within its assigned zone would be destroyed. The Battalion was expected to arrive in Ubao on 17 July, and would prepare to advance to Bunhian."

Meanwhile, Blackburn would establish his command post at the Cadelina Ranch until a Provisional Battalion made up of his Igorot combat company and two other "replacement" companies arrived there. He wanted to move them up to Bunhian. This Provisional Battalion would be commanded by Blackburn's S-3, Deogracias Caballero. "Caballero's battalion would be moved south in trucks along [Highway 5] to Masarat Grande. There it would cross the Magat River and march to the Cadelina Ranch . . . .Caballero's battalion would then march west to Ubao." Once there, it would meet up with the other battalions and move north to Mayayao.

At this juncture, Blackburn decided to relieve Dumlao of his battalion command. He had never fully trusted the Longhair chief since his banditry in the lowlands. And the Longhairs' disappointing performance at Tuguegarao only worsened their reputation among the Regimental Staff. Don decided to replace him with Captain William Burch, the *mestizo* S-4.

On July 15, 1945, the Battle for Mayayao began. Commanding the Longhairs, Burch pushed his battalion as far as Ubao, where they came upon a Japanese regiment. Taking the enemy by surprise, Burch's battalion killed over 500 Japanese, captured 200 more, and described his own casualties as "negligible." Meanwhile, Dunuan continued north to Bunhian but got sidetracked by an enemy firefight in Natonin. The firefight, however, soon escalated into a full-scale battle, and Blackburn started to worry. His orders to Dunuan had been to avoid enemy contact and proceed to Bunhian. Now, Dunuan was wasting time and ammunition on a sideshow battle that didn't factor into the XIV Corps strategy.

Aware that he was losing momentum, Blackburn adjusted his plan. He ordered Caballero to take the Provisional Battalion and, with the Igorot combat company in the lead, push through the Japanese defenses around Bunhian. As ordered, Caballero set out on the mountain trails and, despite enemy machine gun and mortar fire, the Provisional Battalion made it to Bunhian. By July 25, Blackburn recalled that except for a few snipers, "Bunhian was secured by the Provisional Battalion and the Advance CP [command post] of the regiment established thereat. At 1700 [5:00 pm] Company K and two platoons of Company M [both from Dunuan's battalion] arrived from Natonin, having fought their way through the Japanese in that area. The Provisional Battalion Commander was ordered to have the [Igorot] Combat Company push toward Mayoyao as a reconnaissance in force in attempt to find out the actual situation in that area. The remainder of the Battalion with Company K and the two platoons of Company M attached would be prepared to advance on Mayoyao on 26 July with the mission of seizing the town.

"The Battalion, the two platoons of Co. M, which were to be attached to the Combat Company, would advance west along the

Bunhian-Mayoyao, from which point they would attack the town. This trail being the most direct and easiest route to Mayoyao, the Provisional Battalion could expect resistance en route. There was another trail to Mayoyao that was known by few others than the natives. It was narrow, rocky, steep, and ill-defined. This trail led through the village of Diwo and terminated at the village of Chaya, which overlooked Mayoyao from approximately 1,100 yards to the Northeast. Company K, which was made up of Igorots, was assigned this route of advance."

The Provisional Battalion left Bunhian on the morning of July 26 and picked up their attachments before settling onto a nearby ridge east of Mayoyao. Meanwhile, Company K marched up the trail to Chaya and entered the town uncontested.

"Company K," Blackburn recalled, "was ordered to attack the town from its commanding position, and at about 0700, 27 July the Company began the descent on the town supported by fire from the Battalion deployed along the ridge. Almost immediately Company K was detected and began receiving fire from the town, but by utilizing the concealment afforded by the contours of the rice terraces and the naturally irregular terrain, the Company was able to continue its advance. Upon reaching a point approximately 300 yards from the town, an enemy machine gun and rifle, located on a knoll to the Company's right flank, opened up killing the Platoon Leader and several men of the leading platoon, who had sprung up and were rushing across the rice terraces toward the town. This caused the Company Commander to halt the assault. During this halt, the enemy was able to recover sufficiently from their surprise and place enough fire on the Company to pin it down." Throughout the morning, Company K tried to push the Japanese back, but to no avail. Pounded by mortar and machine gun fire, they withdrew back to Chaya and rejoined the Provisional Battalion atop the ridge.

From July 27–28, the Japanese defense was the most vicious Blackburn had ever seen, but by the morning of August 1, it appeared as though the tables were turning. Two of Blackburn's battalions had gained the key terrain around Mayoyao, including the ridges that formed the tip of the "bowl" surrounding the town. From these vantage points, they began launching mortars onto the Japanese defenses within the town. Blackburn then called in an airstrike that firebombed the trenches and small cave networks that the Japanese had built around the mountainous city. On August 4, Blackburn called up his 3rd

Battalion from Bunhian to affect the final assault on town. By the morning of August 9, all three battalions, under the cover of P-38 air support, stormed the last of the Japanese trenches and secured the town of Mayoyao.

After the pacification of Mayoyao, Blackburn spent the next few days processing Japanese POWs and sending updates to Volckmann. But suddenly, on August 14, 1945, Don received the greatest news he had heard in four years: the war was over. Japan had surrendered. The news of V-J Day was broadcast throughout the Commonwealth and, later that day, a Japanese delegation carrying a white flag approached Blackburn's headquarters. The leader of the group identified himself as General Mikami's Chief of Staff. The Chief of Staff was a ghastly-looking fellow, with a tired face and an eye patch which covered an undisclosed ocular condition. The Japanese officer didn't say much throughout their meeting, but pulled out a map which he sat on the table in front of Blackburn. The map showed North Luzon and the Japanese dispositions in the Cagayan Valley. Blackburn noticed a large red circle around Tuao and asked the bedraggled officer what the red circle meant.

"Guerrilla Headquarters," he replied.

But if the Japanese knew where he was, why didn't they attack him in Tuao? The Chief of Staff said that there were just too many guerrillas. By his estimate, there must have been over 10,000 guerrillas along the west bank of the Cagayan River.

Blackburn looked up from his map and told him, "I was the guerrilla leader in Tuao. I never had more than two battalions there at any time." The Japanese officer was speechless.

After the Japanese surrender, Blackburn turned his guerrilla force over to Major Eugenio Balao to oversee its conversion into a regular Philippine Army regiment. Meanwhile, the citizens of Tuao organized a Victory Day celebration to coincide with Blackburn's twenty-ninth birthday: September 14, 1945. The celebration began with the ringing of the town's church bells and a great feast in the Tuao plaza. Blackburn was surprised to see that community leaders from every part of the Cagayan Valley had come to partake in the festival. As the crowd gathered to honor their leader, Don Blackburn gave what would be his last speech as a guerrilla commander. He thanked the people for their

Don Blackburn on V-J Day, 1945. The Donald D. Blackburn Collection

loyalty, bravery, and most of all, their trust. They had fought so fiercely that the Japanese thought there had been 10,000 guerrillas on this side of the Cagayan. "A guerrilla army," he told them, "is a people's army. It lives by and for the people and unless it conducts itself properly and fights for a cause that is just, it will fail." To the people of North Luzon, he owed a debt which he could never truly repay.

Four years had passed since his arrival in the Philippines. Donald D. Blackburn had gone from a young, immature lieutenant to a colonel commanding a regiment of the most daring and fearsome men he had ever known. He had escaped from a ruthless enemy, survived near brushes with death, endured numerous tropical diseases, and relied on the kindness and tenacity of strangers. The Filipinos had given much and asked for very little, save their freedom. After four years in the

Russell W. Volckmann. A 1934 West Point graduate, Volckmann escaped with Blackburn into the highlands of North Luzon. As the senior-ranking officer in North Luzon, Volckmann organized the guerrillas into a four-regiment division known as the United States Armed Forces in the Philippines—North Luzon *(USAFIP-NL). The 11th Infantry (aka "Blackburn's Headhunters") was one of these regiments.* The Donald D. Blackburn Collection

Philippines, Blackburn had grown accustomed to the people and their culture. But now the war was over; the Allies had won and it was time to go home.

Two weeks later, Blackburn bid goodbye to the friends he had made in North Luzon: Tamicpao, Kamayong, and the entire 11th Infantry Regimental Staff. Together with Bruno, Emilio, Barris, and Herb Swick, he drove down to Manila to meet a C-74 Globemaster sent to pick up some high-ranking officers who had been POWs. Once on the tarmac, Blackburn turned for one final goodbye to his mini-entourage. Sharing hugs and handshakes with his brothers-in-arms, Blackburn had tears in his eyes as he boarded the plane.

But upon his return to the United States, Don discovered his greatest victory. After four years, Ann Smith was still waiting for him.

Colonel Blackburn, 1945. At the age of twenty-nine, he was the youngest Colonel in Army history. The Donald D. Blackburn Collection

CHAPTER 9

NEW BEGINNINGS

D on Blackburn returned home on September 17, 1945. There were no crowds, no cameras, no ticker-tape parades—just the kind of fanfare he had hoped to avoid. The past four years had been the most chaotic of his life. The only thing he wanted now was to get back to his family, and the girl he left behind. The interceding years had been particularly hard on Ann Smith. After the fall of Bataan, Don had been designated "Missing in Action"—a status that the War Department would not lift until the spring of 1945. For nearly three and a half years, Ann held on to every last bit of hope she had, praying that Don was still alive. On the tarmac at the airport in Columbus, Georgia, however, Ann reunited with her long-lost beau. They were married on December 4, 1945.

Before Don could return to his normal life, however, the Army put him through a series of reintegration programs: "the hospitalizations [for his tropical diseases], the check-ups, and then, the POW orientation courses." Although Blackburn had never been a prisoner of war, "all the POWs, and most of us who had been guerrillas," he said, "were put on orders to attend this course." The POW Reorientation Program was held at five different Army posts: Fort Benning, Fort Bliss, Fort Knox, Fort Sill, and Fort Riley.

"This course," Blackburn said, "was designed to reintroduce us to the Army's modern equipment" and to reintegrate them into the Army culture. "During this orientation, we'd go from camp to camp," and

*Ann Smith and
Don Blackburn
on their wedding
day, December
4, 1945.*
The Donald
D. Blackburn
Collection

Blackburn's group included none other than Colonel John P. Horan—the same officer who had led Blackburn's column into Baguio in 1941. Despite the incendiary comments Horan had made against the US as a POW, Blackburn claimed, "I had no feelings for or against him." After all, the war was over and, as far as Don was concerned, the Vichy-ite comments "were water over the dam."

His feelings for Horan, however, were about to turn ugly.

"During the orientation visits," Don explained, "we would sit on the bus and talk about what went on over there [in the Philippines]. I gave him a pretty good rundown to include the execution of [Hillary P.] Clapp," the provincial governor who had collaborated with the Japanese and who was, coincidentally, an old friend of Horan's. "I had given Horan all the details on this because he had asked me.

"Well, lo and behold," Blackburn continued "one day I got a letter from the IG [Inspector General] of the Army," implicating him for the

Blackburn with his POW re-orientation class at Fort Bliss, Texas, 1946. Blackburn stands in the back row, fifth from the right. The Donald D. Blackburn Collection

murder of Hillary Clapp. *Don was furious.* Horan had surrendered to the Japanese, made treasonous statements against his country, encouraged other USAFFE personnel to surrender, and was now criminalizing a fellow officer for executing an enemy conspirator.

Blackburn fought with the Inspector General's office over the next several weeks, but the case was ultimately dropped as the execution was deemed appropriate for military security. However, it would not be the last time that Blackburn (or his comrades) would have to defend themselves against accusations of war crimes.

After the POW Reorientation ended in July 1946, Blackburn went to Washington in search of a new assignment. Roaming the halls of the Pentagon he said, "I was looking for a job. This may sound strange and you may wonder why I wasn't assigned a job. But there I was, a 29-year-old guerrilla colonel," and no follow-on orders for a new assignment. It was indeed peculiar that Blackburn hadn't been given a new assignment, but the Army of 1946 was in a state of flux. Due to the rapid demobilization and downsizing, the postwar Army struggled to find and create billets for those who remained in uniform.

Luckily, Blackburn found someone willing to take him on. He spoke to the Commanding General of the Military District of Washington (MDW) who appointed him the District Provost Marshal and G-2 (Chief of Intelligence). "Not that I knew anything about being a provost marshal," Blackburn said, "but here I was," ready to tackle the problems of a postwar Army. As the MDW Provost Marshal, Blackburn commanded a Criminal Investigation Detachment and one Military Police company.

Blackburn recalled that it was an interesting time to be in Washington. As the 8,000,000 men in Army khaki came home, "one of their discharge points was Fort Meade, Maryland," which fell under Blackburn's jurisdiction. During the week, they would be confined to the base to complete their out-processing. However, on the weekends, they would come into Washington and cause no end of trouble for the MPs and the DC Police. "The MPs had a real merry time in town, trying to police up the service types who were exuberant over getting out. This was quite a town." Essentially, the returning servicemen would get loud, drunk, and engage in colorful antics that the local populace didn't find amusing. Blackburn even recalled one incident where "the MPs picked up a GI and a WAC [a member of the Women's Army Corps] who were 'enjoying each other' with more than a just a cordial relationship under a bush in front of the Pentagon. The MPs put them in the brig at Fort Myer." Blackburn's days as the Washington Provost Marshal were filled with stories like this.

And in the middle of it all, Don—like many of his contemporaries—had to accept an involuntary reduction in rank. Attempting to normalize its postwar rank structure, the Army compiled a list of every officer who had received a wartime promotion and demoted them by one, two, or as many as three ranks, depending on merit, time in service, and their overall contribution to the war effort. Blackburn was fortunate in that he was only reduced to a Lieutenant Colonel.

Meanwhile, the Philippine government and the US Army's Philippine-Ryuku Command had begun indicting former guerrillas who had executed enemy spies and informers. Blackburn had already deflected the accusations from Horan, but now several others "were being charged with murder, and those charged were being thrown into courts in the Philippines."

After his own near-brush with the Army legal system, Blackburn wasn't going to let his comrades fall victim to a war crimes witch-hunt. While in Washington, Don paid a visit to General Charles P. Hall, who had commanded the X Corps in the Pacific theater. Don explained that there should be no reason why *any* serviceman should stand trial for eliminating spies and saboteurs. To Blackburn, enemy conspirators belonged in the same category as the Japanese themselves. Hall replied, "I'm familiar enough with what went on in the Philippines, and I'm certainly not in sympathy with this." Hall then forwarded Blackburn's compliant to Army Chief of Staff General Eisenhower, who in turn contacted Russell Volckmann.

When Volckmann corroborated the story, Eisenhower sent him back to see General MacArthur, who had since taken command of the US Occupation Force in Japan. "Ike wrote a note to MacArthur which Volckmann carried, saying that he felt these cases should be quashed." When Volckmann arrived in Tokyo, MacArthur sat him down in his office at the Dai-Ichi Building.

Don and Ann enjoy a quiet afternoon together in the suburbs of Washington DC, 1946. With four years of war and separation behind them, the newlyweds were glad to spend their time this way. The Donald D. Blackburn Collection

"Russ, tell me what the problem is," he said.

Volckmann explained the situation to MacArthur, saying that there should be no reason for anyone to stand trial for eliminating enemy spies. Afterwards, MacArthur took out a legal pad and drafted a memo to General James E. Moore, Commanding General of the Philippine Ryukyu Command: "Let Russ Volckmann explain it all to you, and let him write the ticket. I agree that we shouldn't allow these things to continue."

Volckmann delivered the memo to General Moore and also sought an audience with Manuel Roxas, the first Philippine president elected after the war. During the occupation, Roxas had funneled intelligence reports to the Allied guerrillas while working in the Japanese puppet government, "so he was a good friend of Volckmann's," Blackburn said. Together, Roxas and Volckmann produced an amnesty proclamation that read: "Any act performed in furtherance of the resistance movement should be exonerated."

Although the amnesty act exonerated the Americans involved, it had mixed results for the Filipinos. "It was recognized," Blackburn recalled, "that a lot of Filipinos were being pulled into the courts, which was costing them [the Philippine government] a lot of money. So they set up amnesty boards which were to go around the country and hear the charges that were being levied against Filipino officers and men. The accused would go before the amnesty board, and if it looked as though their actions were in furtherance of the resistance movement, then amnesty was granted."

But as Blackburn admitted, the system was flawed. For example, if a Filipino was charged with executing a collaborator and replied, "Yes, I did it because he was an informer," that was enough to exonerate him. However, if he said, "I was directed to execute him by Captain John Smith [hypothetical name]. I was carrying out his orders," or some other phraseology, the case would be thrown to the Philippine courts.

Under this system, several USAFIP-NL guerrillas were thrown in jail, and "there was quite a bit of commotion over this. At the time, we were trying to do something about it from this end." Accordingly, Blackburn and Volckmann appealed to the Secretary of the Army, Kenneth Royall, in June 1947. The result of that meeting was a blanket amnesty proclamation for any Filipino who had served under an American commander during the war:

Due to the fact that the military situation in the Philippine Islands, during the period of Japanese occupation, prevented the orders of the recognized guerrilla commanders and their duly appointed subordinates from being confirmed or made a matter of record, all orders of the former said recognized guerrilla commanders as shown by the official records of the United States Army in the Philippines. Such orders having been issued on the grounds of the absolute military necessity for maintaining discipline among their guerrilla forces, and for the security of such forces concerning the elimination of persons aiding or abetting the enemy in the time of war during the period, 8 December 1941, to 15 August 1945, both dates included.

"The next thing we tried," Blackburn said, "was to get this amnesty proclamation, and other depositions sent to the courts on behalf of our people." But the US State Department's legal team claimed that Royall's amnesty proclamation and any related documents were not admissible as evidence due to some jurisdictional conflict.

To make matters worse, Manuel Roxas passed away in April 1948 and his successor, Elipidio Quirino, was none too sympathetic to the guerrillas standing trial. It turned out that Quirino had a relative who had been a low-level commander in USAFIP-NL. According to Blackburn, sometime in 1944, Quirino's kinsman had "pulled his unit into a big warehouse, put a machine gun in the door, called the Japs, and surrendered the whole damn outfit to them."

"Well, you can imagine what ultimately happened to that relative." Blackburn said.

Indeed, one of Volckmann's men shot him; hence, the reason for President Quirino's animosity. However, Ramon Magsaysay, who succeeded Quirino as President in 1953, reopened the cases against the US-AFFE guerrillas. Magsaysay himself had been a guerrilla in Western Luzon and was more receptive to the plights of the accused. Later in the 1950s, Magsaysay met with Don Blackburn to discuss the matter of reopening the cases. At one point, however, the Philippine President told him: "Look so many of these cases of murder were not really aiding and abetting the resistance movement."

Blackburn couldn't have agreed more. He knew that some of his and Volckmann's guerrillas had used the war as an excuse to get rid of

Vacationing in Virginia Beach, 1949. Pictured from left to right are Helen Volckmann, Russell Volckmann, Ann Blackburn and Don Blackburn. The two families remained friends ater the war. The Donald D. Blackburn Collection

their personal enemies. These wayward guerrillas would often settle a pre-war grudge by murdering an enemy and then defending it by claiming the victim was an "informer." The task for Magsaysay, therefore, was to separate fact from fiction. Blackburn never knew the full outcome of the Magsaysay project, although some guerrillas were eventually pardoned.

In the fall of 1947, Blackburn departed Washington to attend the Infantry Officer's Advanced Course at Fort Benning, Georgia. Although the course was designed to prepare junior captains for company command, Blackburn felt he needed to attend. Like many World War II veterans, he had the option of using his combat experience as "constructive credit" for Army Service Schools. "I got a notice that I was to get constructive credit for Fort Benning, Fort Leavenworth [Command and General Staff College], and the Armed Forces Staff College. I was looking down the road and thought, well, I'll need more than constructive credit because that wasn't much help. So I went to Career Management and talked to a Colonel who was running assignments. I told him that I'd like to get one of these schools, just to find out what was going on."

The Colonel replied, "Well, we'll leave the constructive credit on for Leavenworth. We'll send you to the Infantry Advanced Course."

"Fine!" Don replied with a smile.

Thus, as a Lieutenant Colonel, Blackburn enrolled in a class filled with young captains. "I thought that it was the most worthwhile year and an opportunity to get down to the nitty-gritty on those things [company-level tactics] that I had missed." For his seminal project, Blackburn wrote a paper titled "Operations of the 11th Infantry, US-AFIP-NL, in the Capture of Mayoyao, Mountain Province, PI, 26 July–8 August 1945," chronicling one of his battles as a commander in the Philippines. Completing the Advanced Course, Blackburn returned to Washington for a brief tour as the Assistant to the Deputy Chief of Staff for Personnel before being selected as an instructor for the Department of Military Psychology and Leadership at West Point in 1950.

A few years earlier, when General Eisenhower had been the Army Chief of Staff, "he initiated this leadership course at West Point. Eisenhower said that he felt that leadership could be taught, and that he wanted a department in the Academy to do just that." Blackburn was invited at the behest of the Department Head, Colonel Samuel Gee, who "was interested in having about 50 percent of the department being West Pointers and 50 percent being non-West Pointers. They were trying to get a diversification of instructors; people who had been in leadership positions under various conditions." Teaching classes in the art of military leadership, Blackburn imparted his lessons onto a new generation of young officers leaving for the Korean War.

After completing his tenure at West Point in 1953, Blackburn attended the Armed Forces Staff College en route to his new assignment as a NATO attaché in Norway. "I was assigned to the Plans Directorate at AFNORTH—Allied Forces in Northern Europe. This was a very interesting and, I thought, a very productive tour working with other nationalities." Indeed, Blackburn worked for a British General and shared an office with a Captain of the Royal Navy. During his two years at NATO, Blackburn served on the team which revised the AFNORTH Operational Plan—a detailed maneuver and logistics plan for the defense of Northern Europe. It was also during this time that Don and Ann welcomed the arrival of their two children, Donald Jr. (1954) and

*Don and Ann
in Norway, 1953.
Blackburn spent
three years in
Norway as an
attaché to NATO—
Allied Forces
Northern Europe.*
The Donald D.
Blackburn Collection

*A family skiing
trip in Norway,
1956. During
his assignment
to NATO, the
Blackburns
welcomed the
arrival of their
two children,
Donald Jr. (r)
and Susan (l).*
The Donald D.
Blackburn
Collection

Susan (1956). Before he returned to the United States, Don Blackburn was once again promoted to full Colonel.

"My next assignment after Norway was Fort Jackson, South Carolina, as CO [Commanding Officer] of the 3rd Training Regiment," a Basic Training unit. At the time, the Army had set up a new program under the Reserve Forces Act (RFA). "When I came home from Norway, the Chief of Career Management called me in before I went to Fort Jackson and said, 'Look, this is a new experiment. You're going to make it or break it on this job. It's a brand-new approach.'"

Under the RFA, young high school graduates could join the National Guard or Army Reserve, exempting them from the peacetime draft. The program had young recruits train for 20 weeks: eight weeks of Basic Training, eight weeks of Advanced Individual Training, and finally six weeks of unit training. After completing the 20-week program, the young men would go home and fulfill an eight-year obligation to their local Reserve or National Guard unit. Although eight years seemed like a long time, Blackburn noticed that many of his recruits found it preferable to the draft. To them, the motto "One weekend a month, two weeks a year," sounded better than giving up two whole years on active duty—especially since many of these young high school graduates wanted to go to college.

Of course, Blackburn still had to deal with many of the issues that often befell Basic Training units. "These youngsters would be in deplorable physical condition," he said. "Getting them to do a pushup, or pullup, was sort of rare. Like anybody else, they griped about things. But in the long run, they saw that they benefitted from it." Simultaneously, Blackburn initiated a public relations program to reach out to the parents of his young recruits. Every so often, he would fly in a group of parents, let them observe training, and answer any questions they had about their sons' service.

Blackburn also remembered a few "bad apples" who came through his Basic Training program. "One group they sent in, I'll never forget," he said. "It was a whole gang out of Ohio, somewhere along the Ohio/Kentucky border. They were just illiterate. And in addition to that, they were thugs. Man, you talk about problems! Some of the things they did were just unbelievable. It was like a ghetto with all the muggings." All together, there were 16 of these troublemakers from the Ohio group who Blackburn prosecuted and discharged from the Army.

As Commander of the 3rd Training Regiment, Don Blackburn escorts Miss South Carolina during a troop inspection, 1956. The Donald D. Blackburn Collection

Nevertheless, Don enjoyed his year-long command of the 3rd Training Regiment.

In the summer of 1957, however, he received an interesting letter from Washington. His presence had been requested by an organization he had never heard of—the Military Advisory and Assistance Group, Vietnam, headquartered in Saigon.

CHAPTER 10

SOUTHEAST ASIA

The Military Assistance Advisory Group (MAAG) was the command group responsible for all US military advisors in foreign countries. By the time Blackburn arrived in Saigon in 1957, MAAG had been operating in Indochina for nearly a decade. The region had been a French colony from 1887 until the start of the Viet Minh Independence Movement led by Ho Chi Minh in the 1940s. During World War II, Ho Chi Minh had rescued several downed American pilots in Indochina and supplied intelligence on Japanese and Vichy French troop movements. All this, he had hoped, would curry favor with the US government and generate sympathy for the anti-French rebellion. However, Ho Chi Minh had miscalculated America's support for the French and their growing mistrust of all things Communist. After the Viet Minh defeated the French at Dien Bien Phu in 1954, peace negotiations at the Geneva Conference separated Vietnam into two political entities: a northern zone, governed by the Communist Viet Minh, and a southern zone, which became the Republic of Vietnam.

Per the Geneva Accords, the Republic of Vietnam was to hold a reunification election in 1956. However, Ngo Dinh Diem, the South Vietnamese President, cancelled the elections and vowed to stamp out any lingering Communists in the Republic of Vietnam. The Viet Minh who remained in the south (the first incarnation of the Viet Cong) reciprocated by launching a low-level insurgency in 1957.

MAAG had initially been deployed to Vietnam to assist the French in their struggles against the Viet Minh. MAAG personnel were sent to supervise the millions of dollars in US equipment being used by the French. After French forces withdrew in 1956, however, MAAG assumed all major military responsibilities in Vietnam.

When Blackburn arrived in the country, Lieutenant General Samuel T. "Hanging Sam" Williams (who had commanded the 25th Infantry Division during the Korean War) was the current MAAG Chief. At first, Don knew little about the American advisory mission in Vietnam or where he would be assigned. "When you arrived in Saigon," Blackburn said, "you would cool your heels for a few days until he [Williams] decided what to do with you."

After a few days in Saigon, Williams called Blackburn into his office. Their first meeting was one that Blackburn would never forget. "I really liked him, but he was so abrupt and rough that he scared the hell out of his staff." Blackburn recalled him as the type of leader who could be menacing if you didn't understand his mannerisms. Sitting across the desk from Blackburn, Williams said, "Blackburn, I've looked at your record, and by God, it looks like you are just a thief and a crook."

MAAG Headquarters in Saigon, 1955. Blackburn first reported to MAAG in 1957 as the Senior Advisor to the 5th Military Region in the Mekong Delta.
The Donald D. Blackburn Collection

Blackburn didn't know what to make of the comment.

"We've got problems down in the Delta," Williams continued, "and it takes a person like you to get at them. A crook to catch a crook. I'm assigning you there as an advisor to General Quai." Specifically, Williams' orders made Blackburn the Senior Advisor to the 5th Military Region (Mekong Delta).

The first problem that Blackburn noticed was that MAAG's 5th Region headquarters was located in the town of Sa Dec, just north of the Mekong River. General Quai's headquarters, however, was in Can Tho, nearly fifty miles south. Aside from the land distance, the two sites were also separated by the Mekong and Bassac Rivers. This required Blackburn to use the ferry system, "which would take at least an hour or more. I thought that if I was going to be an advisor, then I ought to be near the guy."

MAAG's advisory team in the 5th Region consisted of nine military advisors reporting to the Senior Advisor. Arriving in the Delta, Blackburn met the Senior Advisor he was replacing. Within the first five minutes of their meeting, however, Blackburn could tell that the man wasn't very enthusiastic about the job. His distant and managerial style of leadership had depressed the morale of his subordinate advisors. The 5th Region advisors had been furnished a brand-new tape recorder which the Senior Advisor had commandeered to play his own music. The advisors' barracks also had a built-in bar, but the Senior Advisor had ordered it closed. A Frigidaire and stove had also been imported from the States, but the Senior Advisor would not let his men hook up either one because "they were on a French transformer, and he was afraid it would blow out the stove and the refrigerator." To boot, he had let the Sa Dec headquarters fall into disrepair.

The next day, before relinquishing his duties to Blackburn, the Senior Advisor took him to Can Tho to meet General Quai. When the pair arrived at the General's command post, Blackburn noticed that there was an old French-style villa next door. The structure looked big enough to accommodate the American advisors, and Blackburn asked his comrade why they didn't just occupy the villa instead of the compound at Sa Dec.

"Oh no, you don't want to do that," he replied. "That would disrupt the Vietnamese lieutenants who live there."

"I just let his remark ride," Blackburn said.

The introduction to General Quai was pleasant. Don remembered him as a warm and friendly man with a great sense of humor. As Blackburn was leaving, he turned to Quai and said, "You know, I'll tell you, I'm sitting way up there at Sa Dec, and I can't do you much good up there. How about moving down here?"

"I think that's great," the General replied.

"How about next door?" Blackburn asked, pointing to the same villa the Senior Advisor had tried to dissuade him from.

"Well, that's great, but it's not in very good shape," Quai said. "We'll move those lieutenants out and if you want to restore it, fine, I'd love to have you next door."

The Senior Advisor, however, was incredulous. His fear of offending the Vietnamese lieutenants had just been debunked and he "was really irritated with me," Blackburn said.

The pair returned to Sa Dec, and as the Senior Advisor prepared to leave the following day, Blackburn assembled his new charges outside. "We're going to have a party. Go up and get that tape recorder out of the colonel's room and put it down here on the bar." Blackburn ordered one of his men to hook up the Frigidaire and the stove. He ordered another to get some ice. Meanwhile, Blackburn dusted off the bar and restocked it with wine and other spirits. "The Colonel left there very unhappy with me, but boy, we had a blast that night." Don Blackburn had made his presence known.

The following day, Blackburn began moving his men down to Can Tho and paid a visit to General Quai. "Before I start giving you advice," Blackburn told him, "what's your idea on how to run things down here?" Quai knew the dynamics of the region better than anyone else, and Blackburn wanted to get his assessment before kicking around any ideas of his own.

Quai's appraisal of the 5th Region, however, was dismal. The joint MAAG-South Vietnamese effort to fight the growing insurgency was highly fragmented and crippled by a clumsy, top-down bureaucracy. There was no viable strategy to deal with the Viet Cong, no standardized training curriculum, and many of the units lacked equipment. The 5th Region, like other Military Regions in Vietnam, contained an assortment of ARVN, Civil Guard (South Vietnamese National Guard), Territorial (South Vietnamese Reserve), and Self-Defense Corps (SDC, or local militia) units—all of whom reported to different commanders.

Don Blackburn relaxing on the beaches of South Vietnam, 1957.
The Donald D. Blackburn Collection

Quai's command included two Territorial regiments and joint control of the Civil Guard and Self-Defense units, which he shared with the Province Chief. The 11th AVRN Division was the 5th Region's regular army unit, but it reported to a different set of American advisors, and Quai had no operational control of it. There was "also a Navy unit with river patrol boats, and an Air Force unit that had nothing more than liaison-type aircraft stationed at Sac Trang. All Vietnamese."

Quai was understandably frustrated by the fragmentation. He told Blackburn that he felt the first line of defense against the Viet Cong should be the Civil Guard and the SDC. "If they can't handle it," Quai said, "then we should use the Territorials. The Army [ARVN] should be the last resort." The current scheme of operations, however, was counterproductive. If there was a Viet Cong uprising in a particular province, the Province Chief would call President Diem in Saigon. From there, Diem would dispatch any unit within that province's corresponding Military Region to deal with the problem. Normally, Diem would call up the regional ARVN unit to quell the disturbance, but occasionally he would call up a Territorial or Civil Guard outfit. In those

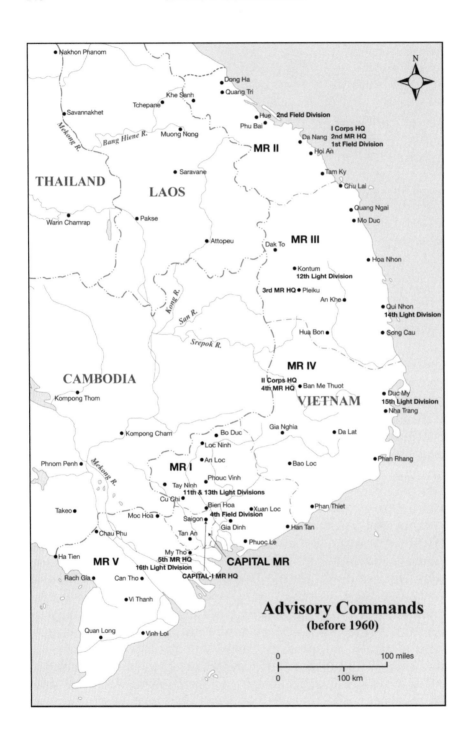

Nakhon Phanom

Dong Ha
Quang Tri
Khe Sanh
Tchepane
Savannakhet   Hue • 2nd Field Division
                                                  Phu Bai   I Corps HQ
Bang Hiene R.   Muong Nong   Da Nang • 2nd MR HQ
                                                                        1st Field Division
                                          MR II   • Hoi An

THAILAND   LAOS   • Saravane   • Tam Ky
                                                                 • Chu Lai

Warin Chamrap   • Pakse   • Quang Ngai
                                                                • Mo Duc

                              • Attopeu   • Dak To   MR III
                                                                        • Hoa Nhon

                                              • Kontum
                                              12th Light Division

                                    3rd MR HQ • Pleiku
                                                    An Khe •   • Qui Nhon
                                                                      14th Light Division
Kong R.
San R.   Hua Bon •   • Song Cau

              Srepok R.

CAMBODIA   MR IV
                                    II Corps HQ
                                    4th MR HQ • Ban Me Thuot
                            • Kompong Thom   VIETNAM   • Duc My
                                                                      15th Light Division
                                                                     • Nha Trang

                        • Kompong Cham   • Gia Nghia
                                          • Bo Duc   • Da Lat
                                        • Loc Ninh
Phnom Penh •   • An Loc   • Bao Loc   • Phan Rhang
                              MR I
                                    • Tay Ninh   • Phouc Vinh
Mekong R.   Cu Chi • 11th & 13th Light Divisions
                                          Bien Hoa •   • Phan Thiet
Takeo •   Moc Hoa •   Saigon • • Xuan Loc
                                        • Gia Dinh   4th Field Division
              • Chau Phu   Tan An •   • Han Tan
                                                      • Phuoc Le
Ha Tien •   MR V   My Tho •
Rach Gia •   Can Tho •   5th MR HQ   CAPITAL MR
                                    16th Light Division
                        • Vi Thanh   CAPITAL-I MR HQ

                                          Advisory Commands
Quan Long •   • Vinh Loi   **(before 1960)**

                        0   100 miles
                        0   100 km

instances, General Quai would never be consulted and he wouldn't even hear about the operation until after it was over. This top-down execution was happening all over Vietnam, and Military Region commanders like Quai were constantly left in the dark.

To complicate matters even further, there were police districts called *arrondissments*—a holdover from the French colonial era. "The boundaries of an arrondissment," Blackburn noted, "would not necessarily coincide with the boundaries of a province. They would cut across several provinces." Sometimes President Diem would relieve a local Territorial or Civil Guard commander and put the arrondissments commander in charge to quell a local uprising. Quai also needed the patrol boats to move his troops along the canals and Mekong River; however, the Vietnamese Navy would rarely grant him access to their watercraft.

Throughout his year in Vietnam, Blackburn farmed out each of his advisors to the Territorial and Civil Guard regiments in the 5th Region. He emphasized training in small-unit tactics and individual marksmanship, topics which he considered vital to building a successful infantryman. Unfortunately, Blackburn's training program wouldn't last—all Territorial regiments were disbanded in 1958. "To me this was a grave mistake," Blackburn said. But MAAG wanted to reorganize Vietnam's light mobile infantry units into heavy infantry divisions. The problem was that "MAAG was restricted by the troop ceiling that had been set by the Geneva Accords." MAAG, therefore, simply went around the issue by converting the Territorial Regiments into ARVN divisions.

According to Blackburn, "The word out, again in Saigon, was that 'Well, those Territorial Regiments were not very well trained anyway.' But neither were the rest of the ARVN forces. It was always my position that we could train the Territorial units as well as we could train the ARVN, and that they could react among their people better than could the ARVN, who were rooting, tooting, shooting, looting, and carrying on all kinds of unacceptable activities when they were patrolling, or on operations in the Delta."

Don also had reservations about the training of the Civil Guard. The Civil Guard, in practice, was a constabulary force whose training was handled by American police officers on contract from the Chicago and New York Police Departments. Blackburn said, "I felt that this was the sort of paramilitary capability that should be developed," but not by US policemen. Security matters in Vietnam were a little more complex than the American tradition of law enforcement.

Moreover, these Civil Guard units rarely travelled outside their compounds. This upset Blackburn because "the Delta was a remote area where there were very few roads. Transportation was by rivers and canals. And if they were going to keep a hand on what the Viet Cong were doing, they had to have people who could get out and patrol around that vast region." Nonetheless, the Civil Guard and SDC units chose to remain in their little *beau geste* forts. "They were sitting ducks for anyone who wanted to attack them," he said. "I left Vietnam with a strong conviction about the training of these local elements to detect and ferret out the Viet Cong, because during that year [1957–58], there were very, very few instances of terrorism."

Blackburn also noticed that there were vast areas of the Mekong Delta that no one—not even the ARVN—would go into. "As a matter of fact," he said, "I crisscrossed the Delta myself in my [jeep] with only my driver and an interpreter because the South Vietnamese Army would not go in there. There was considerable evidence at the time of Viet Cong activity. And you'd get wind of it from the people. This was the time when we should have installed a means of detecting and eliminating their activity, when we could control it with a paramilitary, or police force, rather than relying on the ARVN to do the job. That would leave the ARVN to train for any external threat [i.e. the North Vietnamese Army]."

Despite Blackburn's appeals to the 5th Region staff and the MAAG Headquarters in Saigon, the status quo in Vietnam continued. The cruel irony was that the South Vietnamese were making many of the same mistakes that the Japanese had made in the Philippines. There was no sharing of intelligence, no clear strategy on how to fight the Viet Cong, the Military Region commanders rarely spoke to one another, and the civilians in South Vietnam were often harassed by their own military.

Overall, Blackburn's first tour in Vietnam "was not a very gratifying year."

In the fall of 1958, however, he received another letter from Washington. Don had just been named the new commander of the 77th Special Forces Group at Fort Bragg, North Carolina.

Don Blackburn relished the opportunity to command a Special Forces Group. He had left Vietnam convinced that the US needed a different

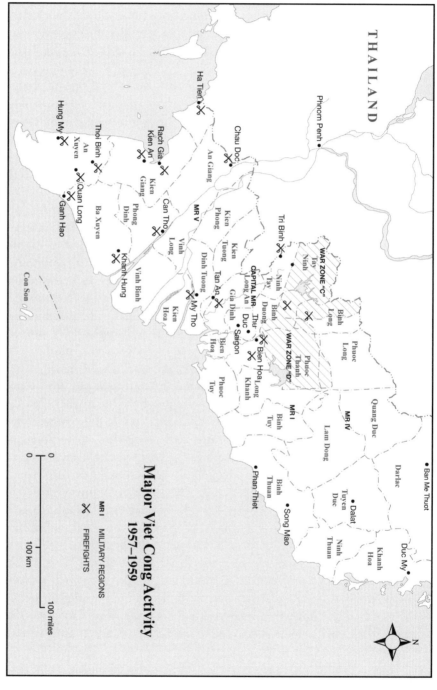

This map depicts all major Viet Cong engagements from 1957–1959. As seen on the map, there were several firefights between the Vietcong and ARVN forces in the 5th Region during Blackburn's tenure.

THAILAND

Major Viet Cong Activity
1957–1959

MR I   MILITARY REGIONS

✕   FIREFIGHTS

N

0   100 km

0   100 miles

Phnom Penh •

Ha Tien •✕

Hung My •✕

Rach Gia •✕
Kien An •

Thoi Binh •

An
Xuyen

• Quan Long ✕

• Ganh Hao

Kien
Giang

Ba Xuyen

Phong
Dinh

Vinh Binh

✕ Khanh Hung

Chau Doc •✕

An Giang

Can Tho •✕

MR V

Kien
Phong

Vinh
Long

Kien
Tuong

Dinh Tuong

Kien
Hoa

Tan An ✕

✕ My Tho

Tri Binh •✕

Tay
Ninh

Ninh
Binh

WAR ZONE "C"

Tay
Duong

Gia Dinh

Long An

CAPITAL MR.
Thu
Duc

Bien
Hoa

• Saigon

✕ Bien Hoa

Long
Khanh

Phuoc
Tuy

Binh
Long

Phuoc
Long

WAR ZONE "D"

Phuoc
Thanh

MR I

Binh
Tuy

Quang Duc

Lam Dong

MR IV

Darlac

Tuyen
Duc

• Dalat

Khanh
Hoa

Binh
Thuan

Ninh
Thuan

• Phan Thiet

• Song Mao

• Ban Me Thuot

• Duc My

Con Son

application of force—the conventional approach to the advisory effort wasn't working. And Blackburn wondered why the US Special Forces Groups had not been more widely used within MAAG. After all, "when Volckmann was establishing the Special Forces, he [Volckmann] recognized from his experiences in the Philippines that the Special Forces trooper and their officers had to have the capability of organizing, directing, training and operating conventional company and battalion-sized units." However, when Don Blackburn arrived to take command of the 77th, he noticed that there was nothing in their training program "that accommodated this requirement. It was ignored because of all the other training requirements that had to be checked off."

To correct this, Blackburn asked the US Continental Army Command if they would give him two basic training infantry companies out of Fort Benning. His plan was to assign a B-Team, and all of its organic A-Teams, to train the companies during the Advanced Individual Training (AIT) portion of their training. The Army agreed and lent Blackburn the two companies on a trial basis. From the beginning, it was clear that the 77th's A-Teams could not handle the mission with the degree of competency that Blackburn thought they should. Nonetheless, training the AIT units gave them a realistic platform for understanding company-level training plans.

Another area in which Blackburn felt his troops should be proficient was infiltration—especially at night. Previously, the 77th had penetrated the Redstone Arsenal in Alabama to test the physical security of the installation. The A-Teams had successfully penetrated the compound and demonstrated Redstone's early vulnerabilities. Inspired by the exercise, Blackburn approached the Governor of the Panama Canal Zone to let his troopers test the security of the Canal. The Governor agreed and Blackburn sent a large contingent to the US Army Jungle Warfare School in Panama to prepare for the mission. To make things easier for the Governor, Blackburn told him that the A-teams would attack the Canal within a very brief time frame. "We gave him almost the exact hour so that he could call up the Reserves, alert the police, and use other US Army units" stationed in the Canal Zone. On the night of the operation, even with the Canal Zone forces on high alert, Blackburn's men successfully penetrated the Panama Canal's security.

Later, Blackburn's men had the opportunity to do the same thing

Don Blackburn as the commander of the 77th Special Forces Group, 1959.
The Donald D. Blackburn Collection

at Camp David. Washington wanted to check the security of the Presidential retreat and asked Blackburn to carry out the mission. Preparing for the operation, Blackburn staked out the vicinity of Camp David, taking notes on the activities of the Marine Guards and the Secret Service. "When the time came to do it, which was during Ike's administration, and while he was visiting Camp David, the troopers went in and dropped a little note in the mailbox that they had been there, and got out." The President was none the wiser until Blackburn went back to the White House for a debriefing the following morning. Needless to say, Eisenhower's staff was shocked. Perhaps in an attempt to save face, the President's staff asked Blackburn to repeat the operation in the winter, when the trees would have no foliage and the SF operators would be easier to spot. Don accepted the challenge and performed the same operation in the dead of winter. The result was the same: Blackburn's men slipped past the Marine Guards, motor patrols, and Secret Service Agents to deliver another note safely within the Camp David mailbox.

Another program that Blackburn initiated was an opportunity to train the Special Forces detachments of the Utah National Guard. "I've always believed that the National Guard and Reserves were an ideal place for Special Forces units." One problem with the National Guard and Army Reserve training was that it was difficult to quickly mobilize their units because their personnel often lived over a large area. "But Special Forces are made up of small cellular units, like the A-Teams. These could easily be formed within a town. It wasn't hard to assemble 9 to 15 people into a training session. General Rich, who was the Adjutant General of Utah, demonstrated what I'm talking about. He and I discussed such a training program."

General Rich wanted to improve the quality of his Utah-based Special Forces units: the 134th and 135th Operational Detachments and the 161st Administration Detachment (all precursors to Utah's current 19th Special Forces Group). Rich promised that if the 77th came to Utah to train his National Guardsmen, he would provide all the logistics and set up a camp for them. Blackburn agreed, saying that "it was a wonderful way to get our winter training accomplished." Rich reactivated Camp Williams, a nearly abandoned World War II post, and housed Blackburn's troopers there from January to March 1959.

Don's first training exercise in Utah was a memorable one. On January 2, 1959, the 77th Special Forces Group was scheduled to make a 1:00 a.m. jump into the Utah countryside. With a fresh blanket of snow covering the drop zone, Blackburn advised his men to pack "Bear Paw" snowshoes for the training event. However, Blackburn's troopers bucked his advice. "Sometimes, you couldn't tell these survival 'experts' what to do. I let them select their own equipment with the thought of testing their know-how. None of them wanted to take the Bear Paws. However, before the exercise, I arranged with the highway emergency people to have a couple of tractors hidden in the woods equipped with ropes. This was necessary because I had told myself that, 'I know we are going to have some trouble.' Sure enough, when they dropped these guys, the fun began."

When his troops landed on the drop zone, they sank into snow— some of them chest-deep. Chuckling, Blackburn let his men thrash around in the snow before throwing them the ropes and pulling them out with the tractors. "From then on, they carried the Bear Paws," he said.

During the week, Blackburn's men would focus on their own training, and on the weekends they would train the National Guard A-Teams rotating in from Provo, Ogden, and Salt Lake City. It was an effective training tool for the 77th Group because it replicated the teaching methods they would use to train and organize guerrillas. But as Blackburn was sharpening the skills of his SF operators, a Communist insurgency was brewing in Laos.

Since 1953, the Royal Laotian government had been fighting against a Communist insurgent group known as the Pathet Lao. Like its neighbor Vietnam, Laos had also been a colony within the greater French Indochina. As French colonial power waned and the Viet Minh were on the rise, a rogue Laotian prince named Souphanouvang joined Ho Chi Minh's organization and brought the Communist ideology back to Laos, becoming the first leader of the Pathet Lao. Meanwhile, a nervous King Sisavang Vong, the monarch of Laos, solicited help from the United States to train his Royal Lao Army.

When Don received the alert that his men would deploy to Laos, he knew that they would have to be well versed in the culture and characteristics of the Laotian people. He subsequently assembled a team of subject matter experts from the Pentagon and the State Department to brief his men on the history and culture of Laos. Simultaneously, he flew to Vientiane (the Laotian capital) to discuss the upcoming deployment with General Johnny Heinteges, chief of the Program Evaluation Office (PEO). Since the Geneva Accords had prohibited any foreign military from establishing bases within Laos, the PEO was a civilian "cover" for the US military mission. General Heinteges and his men even wore civilian clothes to help with the ruse.

In their first meeting together, Heinteges stressed the need for secrecy. Blackburn's men were to come in as "civilians," leaving behind their military IDs and uniforms. The cover story was that they were members of a US Geodetic Survey team. Heinteges wanted the 77th's Operational Detachments "to go out and train the Laotian battalions on site" and the effort led by Blackburn's team was to be codenamed Operation *Hotfoot*—later re-designated Operation *White Star*. Returning to Fort Bragg, Don selected Lieutenant Colonel Arthur "Bull" Simons to command the first wave of Operational Detachments into Laos. Simons had previously served as a company commander in the

6th Ranger Battalion during World War II and fought in the legendary Raid on Cabantuan.

Simons and Blackburn assembled a total of nine A-Teams for the first rotation into Laos. All selected personnel received five months of intensive training. Daily lessons in French and Laotian were mandatory and each soldier was given a copy of the books *Ugly American* and *Streets Without Joy* to read before his deployment. "After about four or five months, we were ready to move out and I made a second trip to Laos. I got the target areas that these teams would move into. I was told that Air America would be on the remote end of the Bangkok Airport to fly the teams into their Laos operational areas."

In mid-June 1959, Blackburn's men loaded their equipment aboard two Air Force C-124s and departed Fort Bragg for Bangkok International Airport. The White Star teams stopped in California for a few days before proceeding to Kadena Air Base in Okinawa. There, the secrecy of the mission was almost compromised when a UN representative from India arrived at the base. It wasn't clear why the Indian representative was at Kadena that day, but he found it odd that a US Geodetic Survey team would require two fully-loaded C-124s for its operation. The UN bureaucrat questioned Blackburn's men at length until he was satisfied with their story. Finally, the team flew into Bangkok where they cross-loaded onto the Air America planes for their insertion into Laos.

During the first White Star rotation, Blackburn's men not only trained the Royal Lao Army, but several groups of indigenous Hmong, Kha, and Yao tribesmen as well. Within the first few months of the operation, Blackburn's A-Teams had set up training sites near each of Laos' provincial capitals and were training hundreds of Laotians against the insurgency. Perhaps the most important operation to happen under "Bull" Simons' ground leadership was the siege of the Bolaven Plateau. South Vietnamese President Ngo Dinh Diem used to say that the plateau was one of the key pieces of terrain in Southeast Asia. Located in southern Laos—where the Laotian panhandle met Cambodia—the Bolaven Plateau was bordered by the Amamite Mountains to the east, "which provided the boundary between Laos and Vietnam."

During Operation White Star, the Bolaven was a hotbed of Pathet Lao activity, and the North Vietnamese later used it as part of the Ho Chi Minh Trail. Don Blackburn and Bull Simons saw the importance of clearing the Pathet Lao from the Bolaven, but there was a disagreement between the PEO and the US Central Intelligence Agency over who should have authority over the operation. Because the PEO and CIA shared jurisdiction in Laos, their operatives often clashed with one another. However, Simons expected a fair amount of trouble on the plateau, and knew that the CIA's paramilitary agents were not equipped to handle the firefight he was expecting. "He insisted," Blackburn said, "that when he deployed his team in there, that he, and not the CIA, would run it. He would be responsible only to the PEO."

Just as expected, when Simons' team hit the Bolaven Plateau, they encountered fierce resistance from the Pathet Lao. Simons had his men dig in along the eastern end of the plateau with their backs to the Amamite Mountains. But after ten days of "touch and go" fighting, the 77th Special Forces had driven the Pathet Lao from the Bolaven Plateau. The White Star teams retained control of the plateau until Laos officially declared its neutrality in 1962. Operation White Star formally ended in July of that year. Both American and Soviet advisors chose to honor the declaration and left the country, but the North Vietnamese continued to send their forces into Laos and fund the Communist

Serving as a technical advisor on the film Surrender—Hell!, *the 1959 film about Blackburn's war in the Philippines, Don stands with Tamicpao and Keith Andes, the actor who portrayed Blackburn in the movie, 1958. The Donald D. Blackburn Collection*

Blackburn with Keith Andes, the actor who portrayed him in the film Surrender—Hell! *This photo was taken during a small publicity tour preceding the film's release in July 1959.* The Donald D. Blackburn Collection

insurgency there. Blackburn later remarked that "those of us who were familiar with the area agreed that if we had been able to hold the Bolaven during the Vietnam conflict, it would have been much more difficult for the North Vietnamese to use the corridor down through Laos into Vietnam."

During the Laotian deployment, Blackburn was recalled to MAAG Headquarters in Saigon by General "Hanging Sam" Williams. "Williams was looking for a solution to the politically sensitive problem of introducing American military advisors to improve the Vietnamese training in the military regions."* Although US advisors had been active in Vietnam for the past decade, their role had been limited to staff functions, and President Diem was reluctant to have any Americans directly training his forces. By 1960, however, Diem had concluded that the need for American expertise outweighed the political complications, and asked Williams to organize and train a South Vietnamese counterinsurgency force comprised of soldier taken from the ARVN. Williams happily assigned the task to Don Blackburn.

Don seized the opportunity to reiterate the shortcomings he had found in the US advisory mission and the Vietnamese defense structure. He prefaced his memo to General Williams with the observations he had made in the 5th Military Region a year earlier. Essentially, Blackburn said that the Vietnamese couldn't shoot, couldn't patrol, knew almost nothing about small unit tactics, and were poorly led. He then outlined an eight-week training program based on the US Army Ranger model, and added emphasis on field communications, patrolling tactics, reconnaissance, defensive operations, marksmanship, and interrogation.

When he delivered the plan to MAAG Headquarters, General Williams said, "Don, I can't live with an eight-week training program; have you an alternative?" Blackburn replied, "Yes, I can give you a satisfactory program for four weeks, if you agree to 432 hours of training. That's around the clock with no holidays, and no weekends." At first, Williams thought it was unreasonable and that Diem would never sign off on it. But Blackburn reminded Williams that if the Americans could do it, so could the Vietnamese. Blackburn's second condition was that they establish three training camps and that the US advisors (consisting of Army Rangers and Special Forces operatives) retain control of the camps' administration and training. "This included weeding out those who were determined to be inept for the training during the initial selection," Blackburn said, "as well as weeding out those who just couldn't cut the mustard as we went along." Williams still had his doubts, but "when he did put all of this to Diem, the number of training hours, the operation and command of the camps and their training, and the weeding out process, Diem bought it 100 percent."

---

*Finlayson, Kenneth. "Donald D. Blackburn." Veritas, Vol. 4, No. 3, November 2008.

In May 1960, the ARVN Ranger camps were established at Da Nang, Song Mao, and Nha Trang. "Hanging Sam wanted a lieutenant colonel to head a 15-man team per camp. So it turned out that I had one lieutenant colonel and two majors at the time. This is how it was set up, a 15-man team headed by those three field grade officers." Even though the Americans would have operational command of the camps, Blackburn wanted a South Vietnamese counterpart for each one of his officers. The Americans would make the decisions regarding the camp's daily operations while the Vietnamese troop commanders would act as enforcers and executors of the American training agenda. If there were any disciplinary issues with an ARVN soldier, Blackburn would let one of Vietnamese officers handle the punishment.

When the ARVN Rangers graduated the program and joined their Ranger units, "they were preparing the operational orders, evaluating the intelligence, establishing the missions, and analyzing what the missions were going to be" without any assistance from their American advisors, Blackburn said. By 1962, the Vietnamese Ranger companies had been organized into counterinsurgency-focused "Special Battalions," and as the war dragged on, their focus shifted from counterinsurgency to light infantry operations. Nevertheless, throughout their operational history, the ARVN Rangers had one of the best reputations in Vietnam. In 1961, after Blackburn had been reassigned to the Research and Development branch of the Pentagon, he came across two reports submitted by two Marine Corps advisors in Vietnam. Addressed to the Commandant of the Marine Corps, the advisors said, "We have not seen any better trained or led units than were the Vietnamese Ranger companies that had been undergoing training by the American Special Forces teams."

Don Blackburn relinquished his command of the 77th Special Forces Group in the summer of 1960. That fall, he attended the National War College and became head of the Special Warfare Office under the Director of Developments—a branch of the Office of the Chief of Research and Development at the Pentagon. The Special Warfare Office "started out with just myself and four other officers," Blackburn said. "This was about the beginning of the counterinsurgency era. Kennedy was in the White House. Counterinsurgency, limited war, sub-limited war, and other such phrases, were the prevalent descriptors of low-level conflict at the time." Don noted that it was a very interesting time in the Pentagon because "they were trying to get a handle on the operational side of how to go about this business of counterinsurgency."

As chief of the Special Warfare Office, Blackburn drew up the concept for the US Army Land Warfare Laboratory (LWL). Established at Aberdeen Proving Ground, Maryland, LWL tested and evaluated numerous pieces of equipment the Army had acquired for counterinsurgency warfare (for example, night vision devices and the PRC-64 radio). Blackburn remained in the Special Warfare Office until 1965, when he received orders that led to the most critical assignment of his career.

ARVN Soldiers train at the Nha Trang Ranger Training Camp. Blackburn established three of these camps throughout South Vietnam to provide Diem with an elite commando force. Courtesy US Army

CHAPTER 11

SOG

O n January 24, 1964, the Joint Chiefs of Staff created the Studies and Observations Group (SOG), a joint special operations task force consisting of personnel from the Army Special Forces, Navy SEALs, Air Force, Marine Force Recon, and the CIA. Codenamed *Operation Plan 34 Alpha,* SOG was the US military's answer to the fledgling special operations campaign in South Vietnam. Previously, the CIA had taken the lead in most matters of unconventional warfare in Indochina. "One of the most intractable problems confronting the U.S. and South Vietnamese armies was an inability to gather intelligence on North Vietnamese Army (NVA) movements and to interdict the support to the Viet Cong via the Ho Chi Minh Trail."*

SOG's roots began, in earnest, in 1960 with the CIA spy mission led by William Colby. A former Army officer and veteran of the OSS, Colby had parachuted into France during World War II as part of Operation Jedburgh, an Allied mission to lead local resistance fighters in guerrilla warfare against the Nazis. After Colby arrived in Saigon as the new CIA Station Chief, he decided to take a more proactive stance against the NVA and their incursions into South Vietnam. In the spring of 1961, Colby received authorization from President Kennedy to begin sending agents into North Vietnam, first by junk ships, and then by

---

*Finlayson, Kenneth. "Donald D. Blackburn." *Veritas,* Vol. 4., No. 3, November 2008.

aerial insertion. Over the next three years, twenty CIA teams (consisting mostly of North Vietnamese defectors) were air-dropped into enemy territory. However, most were captured by the NVA or otherwise "lost" behind enemy lines.

While Colby's CIA teams ventured into North Vietnam, however, American Special Forces were participating on another front in the secret war, training the ARVN 1st Observation Group (OG) at Nha Trang. The 1st OG was an airborne unit and although considered elite by ARVN standards, they were nothing more than a ceremonial guard for President Diem. Throughout the early 1960s, the 1st OG launched over forty reconnaissance missions into Cambodia, in search of the ever-expanding Ho Chi Minh Trail. However, after two years of combing the Cambodian wilderness, these Observation Group commandos could find nothing useful to observe. Other US Special Forces teams, like those from the 1st Special Forces Group, trained Montagnard tribesmen as scouts and raiders in the Central Highlands of South Vietnam. The term *Montagnard* was French for "people of the mountain." The French colonial government used the term to describe the Buhar, Koho, Jarai, and Rhide tribesmen of the Central Highlands. Unfortunately, early experiments with the Montagnard proved inconsequential and the NVA continued to expand its logistics operations along the Ho Chi Minh Trail.

In 1962, MAAG-Vietnam was officially dissolved and replaced by the Military Assistance Command—Vietnam (MACV).* The following year, realizing that the military needed a wider berth to conduct special operations, Secretary of Defense Robert McNamara approved the plan to create MACV's first SpecOps unit. The result was the JCS's creation of SOG in early 1964. At first, there was such a tight lid on SOG and its operations that only General Westmoreland and a handful of high-ranking officers in the MACV Headquarters knew of its existence.

SOG's first commander, Colonel Clyde Russell, a longtime SF veteran, organized the unit along the lines of the OSS, complete with air, seaborne, and psychological operations sections. SOG received the bulk of its logistical support from two Okinawa-based locations: the CIA station at Camp Chinen and the specially-created Counterinsurgency Support Office. Every bit of equipment slated for SOG use, however,

---

*Pronounced "mack-vee."

SOG
Headquarters
in Saigon.
Courtesy
US Army

was shipped into theater under different auspices—weapons, uniforms, and rations were put in containers with vague and nondescript labels so that nothing could be traced back to the US military.

Throughout its inaugural year, SOG performed several covert operations against North Vietnam. However, aside from a few maritime operations (including one coastal raid that destroyed two NVA radar stations on Son Me and Tung Ngu Islands), none of SOG's early missions yielded anything of great consequence. To make matters worse, after the "Gulf of Tonkin Incident" in August 1964, when North Vietnamese attack boats fired on the *USS Maddox* near Son Me Island, President Lyndon Johnson hamstrung SOG operations by subjecting them to even more presidential oversight—and a full review of every mission before it even got off the ground. Johnson's decision had to have come as a shock to everyone within SOG. After all, the Gulf of Tonkin Incident had been publicized by the US media; and Congress had given Johnson a virtual *carte blanche* for his military plans. Deniability and top-down management, therefore, should have gone out the window. Nevertheless, both Johnson and McNamara stressed the need for secrecy.

That summer, McNamara revisited the issue of sending reconnaissance teams into Laos. He wanted ARVN to take the lead, employing their own teams trained by American Green Berets. During a meeting in Saigon, however, a senior-ranking Special Forces officer warned Mc-Namara that ARVN reconnaissance missions could be successful if, and only if, they were led by American Special Forces.

The Secretary of Defense balked at the proposal. McNamara refused to let any Americans venture into Laos or North Vietnam. He further ordered the reconnaissance teams to be ready to deploy within thirty days. McNamara's hasty reconnaissance program—codenamed *Leaping Lena*—was administered by the CIA with operatives from the 5th Special Forces Group training the ARVN recon scouts. In total, *Leaping Lena* produced five recon teams with eight Vietnamese paracommandos to each team. With pre-selected drop zones along Laotian Highway 92, all eight *Leaping Lena* teams were inserted between June 24 and July 1, 1964.

However, of the forty ARVN commandos who departed with *Leaping Lena*, only four returned. All eight teams were intercepted by the NVA and most of their personnel either killed or captured. But the four shell-shocked commandos who made it back to South Vietnam reported the same thing: a vast network of trails over which the enemy was carrying arms, ammunition, and other materiel into the South. But what the US military, the CIA spooks, and government official like Mc-Namara found puzzling was that these supposed trails couldn't be confirmed by aerial reconnaissance. The North Vietnamese had indeed done a better job of concealing their trails than the US had realized.

In the wake of the disastrous *Leaping Lena* project, it became clear that the US needed a different approach to the secret war in Southeast Asia. Everyone within MACV knew that something was going on in

South Vietnamese Leaping Lena *operatives, though well-versed in the art of camouflage, were poorly-trained and ill-equipped for the reconnaissance missions into North* Vietnam. Photo by William Ewald. Reprinted from *SOG: A Photo History of the Secret Wars* with permission from the Paladin Press.

Laos, but no one was entirely sure what. However, in May 1965, two months after America committed the first of its combat troops to Vietnam, Don Blackburn took command of the Studies and Observations Group.

"To enhance and expand operations," Blackburn said, "I put in a study for cross-border operations designed to focus on a more immediate problem—the infiltration coming down from the North." To accomplish this, he devised a program for "training teams that could infiltrate across the border . . . along the Ho Chi Minh Trail area. This became known as Operation *Shining Brass*." As Blackburn explained it, "This was a three-phased program. The first phase was to introduce small reconnaissance teams into Laos to locate the NVA routes, the infiltration and re-supply routes in the mountainous area of the Amamite Mountains, which was the dividing line between Laos and South Vietnam. The second phase was to train . . . what we called an exploitation force. These units were to be company-sized, and were to be used when we could indentify way stations or other targets that were appropriate for elimination by a larger ground force.

"These companies were to be comprised of Nungs, that is, they

Blackburn's first portrait as the commander of the Studies and Observations Group (SOG), 1965. The Donald D. Blackburn Collection

SOG Unit Insignia. Throughout its existence, SOG was also referred to as MACV-SOG and MACSOG. The Donald D. Blackburn Collection

were people of Chinese origin from the Yunnan border of China who had moved south during the French confrontation in the north. They were fairly well trained, and there were a lot of them around the Saigon/Cholon area who were no longer in the Vietnamese armed forces. This was our source of recruitment. The third phase was to move into the area of Laos and organize the natives."

Other native groups who trained for the *Shining Brass* operations were the Montagnard and the Kha. "We organized these people into guerrilla units which were to be employed against the southern infiltration of the North Vietnamese. By doing so, we would deprive the [NVA] of the personnel that they were using as porters, suppliers of food, and providers of comfort."

But with the memories of *Leaping Lena* still fresh in their minds, the JCS and the Chief of the US Pacific Command (CINCPAC) didn't look favorably on Blackburn's new program. Whereas *Leaping Lena* relied exclusively on South Vietnamese operatives, SOG proposed inserting teams of nine Vietnamese troopers (Montagnard, Kha, Nung, etc) led by two or three American Green Berets for recon missions into Laos. All native tribesmen would receive parachute training as well as extensive classes in marksmanship and demolition. "After several months of negotiation," Blackburn said, "with the JCS and CINCPAC, it [Shining Brass] was approved on 21 September 1965."

Even with approval from the Joint Chiefs, however, *Shining Brass* was beset by political problems. William Sullivan, the US Ambassador to Laos, stepped in and ordered Blackburn to limit his area of operation in Laos. "The US Ambassador naturally was quite concerned since we were going to be operating in his territory. So, where we'd proposed to go up to twenty kilometers deep into Laos, he wanted to restrict that distance of twenty kilometers to about ten. And where we had advocated operating from the Cambodian and Laos border northward to the 17th Parallel, he wanted to designate little chunks of territory where we could operate. It would be ten kilometers deep, and maybe, ten to fifteen kilometers wide." Sullivan designated two such areas, known as "boxes," in which the SOG teams were to operate.

At first, Sullivan didn't even want to allow helicopter insertions, "though he didn't object to them being [extracted] by helicopter." However, after Blackburn explained the need for round-trip helicopter support, the Ambassador relented. To effect his helicopter insertions,

Don Blackburn inspecting the troops at a SOG camp, 1966.
The Donald D. Blackburn Collection

Blackburn tapped a South Vietnamese Air Force (VNAF) unit, the 219th Helicopter Squadron. Equipped with the old but reliable H-34 Kingbee helicopters, the 219th had some of the most fearless pilots in the VNAF.

To lead the initial SOG teams in their reconnaissance missions, Blackburn turned to one of his most trusted friends, Colonel Bull Simons. Accompanying Simons on Blackburn's command team were Lieutenant Colonel Ray Call, Major Charlie Norton, and Captain Larry Thorne. Ray Call was personally selected by Simons to head SOG's field headquarters at Da Nang. Norton, a Green Beret with combat experience in the Korean War, was put in charge of SOG's first Forward Operating Base (FOB) at Kham Duc. FOB Kham Duc was selected because the initial launch site at Da Nang was deemed to be too far from the Laotian border. Soon, two new FOBs would open at Kontum and Khe Sahn. By the end of the war, SOG would have six Forward Operating Bases throughout South Vietnam. Larry Thorne, another one

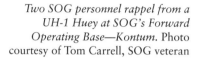

Two SOG personnel rappel from a UH-1 Huey at SOG's Forward Operating Base—Kontum. Photo courtesy of Tom Carrell, SOG veteran

of Simons' personal draftees, was a Finnish-American who fought the Russians in the Winter War of 1940. Thorne was selected as a senior trainer for the first Shining Brass teams.

By October 1965, the NVA was employing nearly 30,000 logistical and support troops on the Ho Chi Minh Trail. And although Hanoi denied it, an estimated 4,500 enemy troops passed through the trail into South Vietnam every month. Meanwhile, the Shining Brass teams trained feverously at Kham Duc. There were five reconnaissance teams for the first wave in Laos—codenamed Alaska, Idaho, Kansas, Iowa, and Dakota. Each team would be led by a specially-selected Green Beret and given the codename "One-Zero." The One-Zero had to be a highly-decorated SF veteran whose bravery, intelligence, and record of service were beyond reproach. He had the liberty to recruit and train his own tribal operators and had considerable freedom in planning the recon mission. A One-Zero had two assistants, also Green Berets: "One-One," the assistant team leader, and "One-Two," the radio operator.

SOG's first reconnaissance mission, executed by Team Iowa, was launched on October 18, 1965. It was headed by a One-Zero named Master Sergeant Charles Petry, and his team consisted of seven Nung tribesmen, one ARVN officer, and a One-One, Sergeant First Class Willie Card. Team Iowa's objective was a portion of Laotian Highway 165, just beyond the South Vietnamese border, about twenty miles west of Kham Duc. US intelligence indicated that the NVA was using the area as a platform for its attacks on Chu Lai and Da Nang. Before the mission could begin, however, Team Iowa had to discard every weapon

Above: *North Vietnamese forces along the Ho Chi Minh Trail, 1965.* NVA Photo.
Below: *A winding portion of the Ho Chi Minh Trail as seen from a SOG Helicopter,*
1966. Photo by Mecky Schuler. Both photos reprinted from *SOG: A Photo History*
of the Secret Wars with permission from the Paladin Press.

The North Vietnamese used every form of transportation to carry supplies over the Ho Chi Minh Trail, including bicycle porters as seen here in 1966.
Captured Enemy Photo. Reprinted from *SOG: A Photo History of the Secret Wars* with permission from the Paladin Press.

and item of clothing that could be traced to the United States. As was common in the world of special operations, SOG wanted complete deniability. Petry and his men were given Asian-made uniforms with no rank or insignia. Their weapons were of Swedish and Belgian manufacture. Should they be caught, Team Iowa's cover story was that they were on a rescue mission to find a crashed C-123 and were unaware that they had crossed the border. Everyone knew it was a weak cover, but to help maintain the fiction, SOG printed up some cartographic maps that intentionally shifted the border about six and a half miles to the west.

Team Iowa took off from Kham Duc in their three H-34s at 6:00 pm and landed in Laos shortly before nightfall. When Iowa landed in the Laotian jungle, they found the stretch of Highway 165 just as they had expected it—NVA everywhere. Still, for the first two days of their reconnaissance, Iowa successfully evaded the enemy, taking note of the NVA base camps, way stations, and trails along the way. On the third

To defend the Ho Chi Minh Trail from aerial reconnaissance and bombardment,
the NVA emplaced several air defense guns in eastern Laos.
Courtesy of The National Archives and Records Administration

day, however, Iowa ran into an enemy patrol. Startled by their unexpected meeting, both sides opened fire on one another, whereupon one Nung was killed. After the brief firefight, Petry's team broke contact and retreated into the jungle with the NVA in pursuit. It was two more days of "cat-and-mouse" before Team Iowa led its pursuers into a target area for an F-105 airstrike which rained fire down on the enemy as Petry and his men were safely extracted by an H-34.

In these early days of *Shining Brass*, Blackburn identified over 500 enemy targets along the Laotian border. With this information in hand, "I asked General Westmoreland, and General Moore, who was then the Seventh Air Force commander, to drop by SOG headquarters so that I could show them the results of this photography." Blackburn showed General Westmoreland the extent of the North Vietnamese infiltration network through Laos. The MACV commander was speechless. "My God, we've got to do something," he told Blackburn. "Can you really see these things?" Blackburn replied that his recon teams hadn't positively identified all of them, but could so by Spring 1966.

By the end of 1965, Blackburn's *Shining Brass* had conducted eight reconnaissance missions into Laos—six of them returning with significant information on the enemy's supply network, caches, and way stations. According to Blackburn's reconnaissance teams, the NVA had done a superb job of concealing the trails from aerial photography. In some cases, NVA engineers had uprooted entire trees from elsewhere in Laos and re-planted them on either side of the Ho Chi Minh Trail. The result was a newly-created canopy to hide their growing network.

Having proved their worth, Blackburn convinced Ambassador Sullivan to ease his restrictions on SOG operations. Beginning in 1966, he allowed Blackburn to widen SOG's operating area to 200 miles along the Laotian border. Blackburn considered this one of his greatest victories while commanding SOG. The Ambassador's previous restrictions on Shining Brass had been frustrating because "having just those two sectors," Blackburn said, "was like throwing a snake into a hen yard. Boy, these people [the NVA] would get all stirred up. Thus, if you tried to put that second team in there, the enemy was alert. Normally,

North Vietnamese engineers build a hasty bridge over a bomb crater in the Trail. NVA Photo. Reprinted from *SOG: A Photo History of the Secret Wars* with permission from the Paladin Press.

after a lapse of time, [the enemy's] lethargy sets in, and you can do an awful lot of things by drawing upon the lethargy of the enemy.

"Our plan was to put a team, say in the southern part of the panhandle [Laotian border] and let it operate, which meant that things would get stirred up. The next team would be put into the north. That would let the south cool off for a while, which invariably it would. Then the third team would be put into the middle. But if you were repetitious in going into any area, you had an alert enemy who provided a nice reception committee."

By the time Blackburn relinquished his command of SOG on July 1, 1966, his operatives had performed 48 reconnaissance missions inside Laos. "I don't think there's any question as to the effectiveness of the Shining Brass Operation," Blackburn said. "It identified and located the so-called Ho Chi Minh 'trail network.' Some people had the idea that it was just a mountain trail. Well, it was a vast complex of trails." But this was just the beginning of the SOG effort. "After I left Viet-

Blackburn inspects another SOG camp near the Laotian border.
The Donald D. Blackburn Collection

nam," Blackburn recalled, "it expanded tremendously." Indeed from these beginnings in 1965–66, SOG's cross-border operations soon expanded into Cambodia and North Vietnam.

SOG continued its secret war against the Communists until the group was disbanded in May 1972. By the end of its eight-year run, the Studies and Observations Group had become the most decorated unit of the Vietnam War. In one company alone, five soldiers received the Medal of Honor. Although the exact number of SOG casualties remains unclear, it is generally accepted that over 300 Americans were either killed or went "Missing in Action" during the SOG missions. Nevertheless, SOG severely disrupted the NVA's activity along the Ho Chi Minh Trail. By the end of the war, SOG operatives had captured or destroyed over 1,000 tons of enemy equipment travelling through Laos and Cambodia. Furthermore, by 1969 SOG had achieved a remarkable kill-to-loss ratio of 150:1 (150 NVA killed for every Green Beret lost to enemy fire).

Despite its illustrious combat history, SOG's operations were largely unknown until the MACV Command History Annexes were declassified in the early 1990s. Although most of SOG's clandestine activities are well known today, it has seldom been recognized that Don Blackburn had such a profound impact on the organization and the direction it took after 1965. In the wake of a failed special operations campaign, Blackburn took the bull by the horns and created a program that, even after he left Vietnam, succeeded in discovering and disrupting the NVA along the Ho Chi Minh Trail.

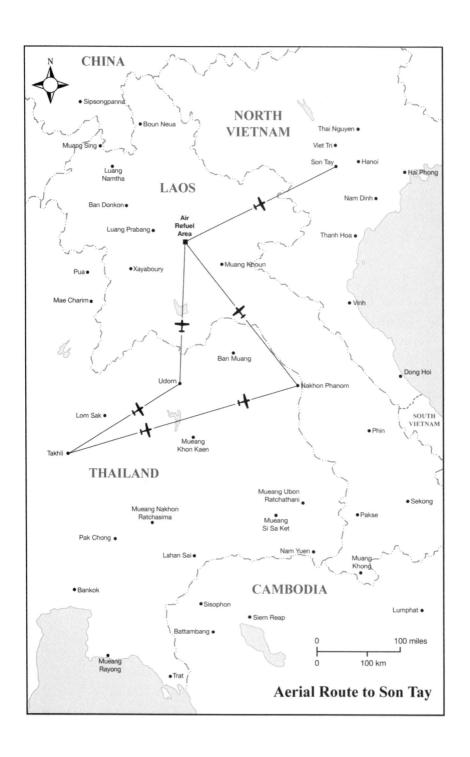

Aerial Route to Son Tay

CHAPTER 12

SON TAY

After Blackburn left Vietnam, he returned for another tour of duty at the Pentagon. He served only a few months with the NATO Planning Group before McNamara drafted him into the Defense Communications Planning Group (DCPG). The DCPG was a research team responsible for the development of the so-called "McNamara Wall." The "Wall" was a series of electronic sensors emplaced along suspected nodes in the Ho Chi Minh Trail. Utilizing what was then "state-of-the-art" technology, the sensors could determine the presence of any human or motorized traffic along the route. From the beginning, Don had his reservations about the project.

"You know, I was never convinced that dropping sensors by air... was going to be too effective. And, it was terribly expensive. To me, it made a lot more sense to go after these targets rather than to try and put a sensor out to see if a couple of Vietnamese from the north were walking along the trail." To Blackburn, McNamara's "Wall" felt like a slap in the face to the SOG teams who had risked their lives to bring back information on the Trail. But alas, Don Blackburn had no say in the matter. Even if his recommendations fell on deaf ears, he had no choice but to let Johnson and McNamara run the war as they saw fit—even if it was to the detriment of the US military. Blackburn left DCPG in the summer of 1967.

His new orders thereafter assigned him once again to Fort Bragg, this time as the Assistant Division Commander (ADC) for the 82nd

Airborne Division. Later that year, Blackburn learned that he had made the promotion list for Brigadier General. "I'd been with the Special Forces for much of my career, and had been to Bragg before. General Seitz was the commanding general of the 82nd, and I guess when he saw my name come up on the [promotion] list, he requested that I be made the ADC . . . and this was indeed a very pleasant year. There was not much movement from Fort Bragg. The assignment just involved training the troops. But one of the interesting periods resulted from the civil disorders around the country—in Detroit and Washington."

Blackburn's tenure with the 82nd Airborne (1967–68) coincided with one of the most turbulent times in American history. Social unrest had taken the country by storm. It was a time of race riots, campus protests, and growing disillusionment with the war in Vietnam. Aside from the National Guard, "the first unit called upon to provide assistance was the 82nd. I personally didn't go to either place [Washington or Detroit]. As ADC, I remained at Bragg and prepared the next group to go if and when they were needed. But I think that the division's conduct during those civil disturbance missions was really a feather in its cap; it did an exceedingly good job."

Because the 82nd Airborne was America's on-call contingency force, the paratroopers received extensive training in riot control and other law enforcement techniques. The paratroops weren't allowed to carry ammunition, but could have their bayonets fixed during the riots. "Discipline was the name of the game," Blackburn said. "For example, in Washington, once the [rioters] saw that the troopers meant business, that they were disciplined in handling problems, and that they were gaining acceptance from the people, things were brought under control." General Seitz would often say to the troops, "Now you go out there, I want fresh starched uniforms every day. I want your helmet with chin straps on. I don't want any fraternization with the civilian crowd. Do your job." And, as Blackburn noted, "They did a very good job." Meanwhile, Don received his promotion to Brigadier General on July 1, 1968.

The riots in Washington and Detroit taught Blackburn much on the importance of civil-military cooperation. "Much depended on command competence and flexibility in dealing with a very fluid and tense situation. They had to block off certain areas and establish control to stop [the] looting, burning, and other disturbances. There was very

Blackburn receives his first star, 1968. He is pinned by his wife Ann and Major General Seitz, the Division Commander. The Donald D. Blackburn Collection

good coordination and cooperation with the 3d Infantry [The Old Guard] and the Metropolitan Police, especially with the police who had intelligence on what was going on, and where it was going on."

But when the 82nd Airborne wasn't fighting crime in the streets of America, it was preparing to fight Communism in the jungles of South Vietnam. In 1968, the Division's 2nd Brigade was alerted for deployment. Blackburn found the task especially challenging as he had to move over 1,000 soldiers into theater in less than 60 days. Coordinating airlifts from nearby Pope Air Force Base, he had to navigate through the myriad of operational and administrative restrictions placed on military flights, including one stipulation that called for "moving the brigade from Bragg through Alaska to Vietnam." But, as Blackburn said, "we really got on target in an adequate time frame."

In early 1969, Blackburn readied himself for yet another assignment. He was told to report to the Chairman of the Joint Chiefs for what

Don Blackburn meets with President Lyndon B. Johnson on the tarmac at Pope Air Force Base during the farewell ceremony for the 82nd Airborne's deployment to Vietnam.
The Donald D. Blackburn Collection

Don Blackburn,
Fort Bragg, 1968.
The Donald D.
Blackburn Collection

Don Blackburn is awarded the Meritorious Service Medal for his role in preparing and training the Division's troops for their deployment to Washington DC and Detroit to quell the ongoing civil disturbances. The Donald D. Blackburn Collection

would be the culminating position of his career: the Special Assistant to the Chairman for Counterinsurgency and Special Activities (SACSA). Essentially a "Special Operations Czar," SACSA was an office that had been set up during the Kennedy years. Most of its activities, Blackburn said, "were devoted to limited war and counterinsurgency, particularly as they related to Vietnam." Aside from the special operations in Vietnam, Blackburn also had to contend with the Overseas Internal Defense Plan. "This was an interdepartmental plan that had been prepared in the late '60s and addressed the instabilities and the need for internal security of countries throughout the world [i.e. those deemed vulnerable to Communist subversion]." The overall responsibility for these countries would fall on the Pentagon staff many echelons above Blackburn, but "when it came to low level conflict involving overseas internal defense planning, SACSA would pick that up."

However, the most memorable event of Blackburn's tenure as SACSA had nothing to do with counterinsurgency. On May 25, 1970, "an Air Force briefing team came to me," he said, "and asked if SACSA could set up a rescue mission using US Army Special Forces personnel" to rescue a select number of POWs in North Vietnam. Two weeks earlier, Air Force Intelligence had determined that there were at least 55 American POWs being held at a place called Son Tay. Twenty-three miles west of Hanoi, the Son Tay Prison Camp had some of the most deplorable conditions of any POW facility in North Vietnam. Its perimeter was bound by a river to the west, barbed wire to the east, and trenches to the north and south. Of the 55 estimated prisoners at Son Tay, the Air Force determined that only five or six of them were in urgent need of rescue. But Don Blackburn didn't agree with that way of thinking. If 55 Americans were expected to be at this camp, why not make an effort to rescue all 55?

"I expressed this view to the Air Force briefing team, and asked that I be permitted to look into it further before giving them a definite answer." The Air Force agreed and "it was at this point that I went in to see the Chairman of the Joint Chiefs of Staff, General Earl Wheeler, and proposed to rescue the POWs." Wheeler was shocked by the proposal. He asked Blackburn how many battalions he would need to accomplish a mission like this. Blackburn's response shocked the General even further.

> I told him that I had no intention of going in there with a battalion. I was going to go in there with a small group of men and helicopters and lift the POWs out.

Still, Wheeler had his reservations. He explained to Blackburn that public opinion of the war had sunk to an all-time low. By and large, the American people resented "any activity in North Vietnam, bombing or otherwise." The US military wasn't winning any popularity contests at home either. Be that as it may, Blackburn told him, something had to be done to shake up Hanoi.

"From my point of view, I wanted to go under any circumstances. For years we had let the North Vietnamese operate in South Vietnam—in Da Nang, Nha Trang, Saigon, and other places. I saw no reason why we shouldn't do the same thing in the north, and I strongly believed that we had the capability to do it. I refused to believe the writings of so many authors [who said] that North Vietnam was a Communist state with highly controlled police methods, methods so effective that you couldn't operate there. Here was an opportunity to demonstrate that

*Blackburn as
the Special Assistant
to the Chairman for
Counterinsurgency
and Special Activities
(SACSA), 1970.*
The Donald D.
Blackburn Collection

we could operate in the heartland of the north and it was no longer their sanctuary. They would have to provide troops to protect their homeland and not send them all to South Vietnam."

After a long discussion, the JSC Chairman said, "Well, Don, if we didn't try this, we'd be against motherhood. We've got to have a good selling point on this. I want you to prepare a briefing for the Joint Chiefs of Staff." Thus Blackburn prepared his briefing for the Joint Chiefs. The war in Vietnam had been hamstrung by political mis-management from the beginning. There had been overcautious rules of engagement, a dubious "hearts and minds" strategy, and too much emphasis on the "hi-tech" versus "boots on the ground." But that was the legacy of Johnson and McNamara. President Nixon and the new Secretary of Defense, Melvin Laird, promised a new approach. Aside from the popular "Vietnamization" program, they eased many of the restrictions that had previously been placed on the US military. For years, the North Vietnamese had played by their own rules: ignoring the Geneva Convention, violating their neighbors' neutrality, and treating American POWs like little more than dogs. The much-heralded peace conference in Paris had stalled, and the POWs were the North's only bargaining chips. As such, now was the time to strike the North Vietnamese in their own backyard.

Wheeler gave his endorsement to the project, but the other Joint Chiefs "didn't want to commit themselves at that point. So, it was suggested that I come up with a feasibility study that I could give them within about a month's time. I was authorized to pull a planning group together." Wheeler was already confident that the project would be a success, but he and Blackburn had to convince the skeptics on the JCS. The planning group that Blackburn pulled together was a 15-man team codenamed *Polar Circle* which convened at the Arlington Hall Station on June 10, 1970. Drawing personnel from the Army, Navy, Air Force, and CIA, Blackburn's *Polar Circle* group determined that the rescue mission could be done and that there were actually 61 POWs at Son Tay. "After hearing the briefing," Blackburn said, "the Joint Chiefs agreed to go with the operation."

Colonel Arthur "Bull" Simons speaks to the Son Tay raiders minutes before they embark on their POW rescue mission. Simons had served in World War II with the 6th Ranger Battalion and led the initial White Star teams in Laos in 1959. JFK Special Warfare Museum. Reprinted from SOG: A Photo History of the Secret Wars with permission from the Paladin Press.

The Son Tay Raid was to have an overall Task Force Commander and a ground commander (the one who led the raiding party on the ground). Since the mission would rely heavily on Air Force fixed-wing and helicopter aircraft, Air Force Brigadier General LeRoy J. Manor was selected to be the Task Force Commander. When the Joint Chiefs asked Blackburn who he would recommend to be the ground commander, he replied "Isn't it obvious?"—referring to himself. "Well, not you! You've got to stay around here and fight the political end of this thing." Such was the JCS's answer. Although disappointed that he wouldn't get to lead the rescue mission, Blackburn once again turned to his trusted friend and colleague, Lieutenant Colonel Bull Simons. Don assigned him the role of ground commander on July 13, and soon thereafter they set up their training center at Eglin Air Force Base in Florida.

Around this time, General Wheeler retired as the Chairman of the Joint Chiefs and was replaced by Admiral Thomas H. Moorer. Briefing Moorer on the latest developments in the projected Son Tay mission, Blackburn progressed to the next phase of the operation. Codenamed *Ivory Coast*, this phase included the training, organization, and deployment of the Son Tay raiders. Moorer, however, made an adjustment to Blackburn's all-star line-up of Special Forces personnel. He made Bull Simons the Deputy Task Force commander and selected Lieutenant Colonel Elliot "Bud" Snydor as the ground commander.

In total, 103 Army and 116 Air Force personnel were selected for the mission. Their numbers included Army Green Berets (many of whom were veterans of SOG), Air Force Para-Rescue, top-rated aircraft maintenance teams, and the most seasoned helicopter and C-130 pilots the Air Force had to offer. The 219 men were told nothing of their destination or the nature of the rescue mission. From the time the Son Tay raiders began training on September 9 to the time they deployed to Southeast Asia on November 10, none of them were permitted any contact with the outside world. They were to have no visitors, no mail, and no telephones.

While Simons and Manor began building their teams, Blackburn busied himself planning out the details of the operation. A nighttime raid, they determined, would be the best option. Reviewing the forecasted weather data for Hanoi, Blackburn and his staff found two "windows" which allowed for the greatest nighttime visibility and conditions favorable for low-level flight. The two date groups were October 18–25 and November 18–25. The staff wanted the October window, which Melvin Laird approved, but National Security Advisor Henry Kissinger delayed the mission. According to Kissinger, the President was not in Washington and could not be briefed in time for an October mission. Thus, Blackburn and his planners defaulted on the November time slot.

The raid was to launch from Udorn Air Base in Thailand. The air armada for the operation consisted of two C-130E Cargo planes, five HH-53C "Super Jolly" helicopters, and one HH-3E "Jolly Green" helicopter—all US Air Force assets. Fifty-six Special Forces troopers would conduct the raid itself. The HH-3E was to carry the 14-man raiding party that would assault the prison compound and extract the POWs. One of the HH-53s would carry a 22-man support team, ready to support the raiding party if needed. Another HH-53 would carry a 20-man security team, to repel any NVA reinforcements or help the other two teams if called upon. Of the three remaining Super Jollies, one was a gunship providing close air support, and the other two were slated for POW extraction. Since the helicopters had no electronic navigation devices, the C-130s would act as aerial guides—leading the helicopters as they followed closely behind in a "Flying V" formation.

Adding to the mission's air support were five A1-E Skyraider jets ready to bring missile fire onto the objective and ten Navy F-4 Phantoms patrolling the airspace for any MiGs in the area. Minutes before the raiders were to reach their targets, Naval air assets from the carriers *Oriskany*, *Hancock*, and *Ranger* would deploy a combined task force of fifty-nine planes for a diversionary attack on Hanoi. At the time, bombing campaigns against the North were still illegal, so the Navy would be dropping flares instead.

In training, the raiders used a full-scale mock-up of the Son Tay prison which the planning staff had reconstructed from aerial reconnaissance photos. Their training tempo started with "dry-fire" exercises during the day and night, followed by "live-fire" exercises, and finally, three "dress rehearsals" at night. By the time raiders deployed to Southeast Asia, they had rehearsed the operation a total of 172 times. Meanwhile the Air Force crews logged over 1,000 flight hours in their C-130, HH-3E, and UH-1H helicopters.

From November 10–18, 1970, the Son Tay raiders deployed to

Aerial photograph of the Son Tay Prison, North Vietnam, 1970. US Air Force Photo.
Reprinted from *SOG: A Photo History of the Secret Wars* with
permission from the Paladin Press.

Southeast Asia and organized their initial staging area in Takhli, Thailand. From there, the entire team was flown to Udorn to begin their final preparations for the mission. Meanwhile, back in the States, Don Blackburn had a problem on his hands. President Nixon had already given Blackburn his approval for the Son Tay Raid. But, at the eleventh hour, Don received an intelligence report suggesting that the POWs might not even be there.

Blackburn was not amused.

Now was not the time to be suggesting that, after months of hard work and preparation, the POWs *may* have been moved to another prison camp.

Stifling his uncertainty, Blackburn purportedly went to Admiral Moorer and told him that, even if the POWs weren't there, the mission must go forward. They would never have this kind of opportunity again. And the North Vietnamese needed to be shown that their backyard wasn't so safe from American firepower. His men were the finest Special Operations personnel in the world; it would be "unforgivable" to cancel the mission after they had put in so many hours of training and preparation. At this point, he would rather execute the mission—and discover the camp empty—than to cancel the mission and find out that the POWs had been there all along.

Thus, the mission went forward.

On the evening of November 18, 1970, Bull Simons gathered his men in the airplane hangar at Udorn Royal Air Base. For the first time, he announced their mission: They were flying deep into North Vietnam to rescue American prisoners-of-war being held at Son Tay, 23 miles west of Hanoi. The men erupted in applause.

The raiders then divided themselves into their three platoons. The 14-man raiding party (codenamed *Blueboy*), would deliberately crash land their helicopter into the compound. The support and security teams (codenamed *Greenleaf* and *Redwine*, respectively) would land along the southern perimeter roughly adjacent to one another. Simons would accompany the *Greenleaf* group while the ground force commander, Bud Snydor, would be on *Redwine*.

The final phase of the operation, codenamed *Operation Kingpin*, was the assault on Son Tay Prison itself. Beginning at 10:00 pm, the aircraft took off from Udorn. Following the trail of their C-130 guides, the heliborne raiders refueled over Laos before making their initial descent over North Vietnamese airspace. A few moments ahead of the raiding party, the HH-53 gunship sprayed the guard towers surrounding the Son Tay Prison. Seconds after the towers erupted in flames, the raiding party, led by Captain Dick Meadows, plowed its helicopter into the compound walls. Springing out of their downed helicopter, Meadows took hold of his bullhorn and announced to the POWs, presumably inside, that their rescue team had come. Meanwhile, Bud Syndor's team had landed at the southern perimeter and killed 20 NVA before linking up with Meadows inside the prison walls. Bull Simons' men, however, landed in the wrong camp. Their HH-53 pilot had mistakenly put them down at a similar camp just a few miles south. Although it was the wrong camp, it didn't stop the enemy there from engaging Simons' men. His 22-man team destroyed a contingent of nearly 100 enemy troops before making their way back to the HH-53. His men arrived at the Son Tay camp a few minutes later.

By this time, Meadows and Snydor discovered that there were indeed no POWs at Son Tay. There were, however, plenty of NVA. Dazed and confused, the North Vietnamese troops tried to rally a counteroffensive, but to no avail. Before they even knew what was happening, the American raiders had already killed thirty of them.

A mere twenty-seven minutes after their insertion, the Son Tay raiders were extracted by their HH-53s (minus the one that was intentionally crash-landed). Evading only a few surface-to-air missiles, the raiders returned to Thailand otherwise unmolested. No POWs had been rescued, but not a single American had lost his life in the Son Tay Prison Raid.

Upon their return to the United States, the raiders' mission was deemed a "tactical success" but overshadowed by what many called an "intelligence failure." As it turned out, the prisoners at Son Tay had been moved to another camp fifteen miles away on July 14, 1970. The reason for their relocation remains unclear, but was likely due to the threat of floods from the nearby river. During the planning and preparation for Son Tay, the US had several reconnaissance assets in Laos and North Vietnam. As early as July–August 1970, ground reconnaissance and aerial photography indicated that the camp was empty. Thus, it raises the question why SACSA didn't know of the prisoners' relocation before November. Some have attributed the failure to a "compartmentalization" of intelligence gathering—meaning pertinent information about the camp never made its way to SACSA and the Son Tay task force. Whatever the reason behind the intelligence failure, these were Blackburn's only comments on the matter,

"After the raid, there were a lot of accusations about the poor intelligence. I feel just the opposite. The intelligence was absolutely superb. On an operation like this, the person who is doing the planning and directing has got to have access to highest level in the intelligence agencies of the government, and fortunately, I did—with the CIA, the DIA, and the NSA.

Yes, the prisoners, were they there or not there? That was tough… if we had agents in Hanoi, it would have helped, but in actuality, we didn't have. So we had to use other sources for determining the status of those camps . . . we used drones, but they can give away the target if they create a pattern by flying over it too frequently. This was the concern of poking and probing around that camp too much. If the NVA ever became suspicious, and our troopers went in there, they would be like sitting ducks."

Nevertheless, the Son Tay raiders were highly decorated for their bravery: six Distinguished Service Crosses, five Air Force crosses, and eighty-five Silver Stars.

The raid was maligned as a failure by the American media and opponents of the Vietnam War. They denounced what they perceived as poor intelligence gathering, and feared that the treatment of American POWs would worsen as result. In fact, just the opposite happened. The North Vietnamese suddenly realized that Hanoi was not invulnerable to American ground troops and, as a result, the treatment of American POWs vastly improved. Blackburn said, "I've had too many remarks made to me by former prisoners, indicating how their lifestyles changed. And, how their hopes were renewed about other possible rescue attempts or release. In my mind, that justifies having given the 'Go' on this operation." Bull Simons later remarked that even if there was a one in ten chance that the POWs were at Son Tay, it was well worth the raid.

EPILOGUE

After the fallout from the Son Tay Prison Raid, Don Blackburn retired as a Brigadier General on July 1, 1971. However, he did not retire in disgrace. At his retirement ceremony in Fort Bragg, North Carolina, the Special Forces community congratulated him for his many years of hard work and dedication. Upon his retirement, Blackburn moved his family to McLean, Virginia, where he began a second career with *Braddock, Dunn, and McDonald* (BDM)—a Washington-based think tank—as their Vice President for Special Programs.

For the next ten years, Blackburn worked on several BDM-sponsored studies and program evaluations for the Department of Defense. He retired for good in 1981 and relocated to Sarasota, Florida, where he remained for the rest of his life. But even in retirement, Blackburn said, "I never find time hanging heavy on my hands. You know, from time to time, there are symposiums and seminar groups that for some unknown reason still send me an invitation."

Don and Ann were married for over 45 years until her passing in 1991. For the next seventeen years, he lived quietly at his home in Sarasota, enjoying, among other things, his life as a doting grandpa. Sadly, in the early 2000s, Don Blackburn was diagnosed with Alzheimer's disease. By the time I visited him in early 2008, the disease had already progressed into its later stages. Donald D. Blackburn sadly passed away on May 24, 2008.

Without qualification, Don Blackburn is one of the most remark-

Above: *Blackburn's retirement ceremony, Fort Bragg, July 1, 1971.*
Below: *Don Blackburn enjoys a humorous moment with President and Madam Marcos in the Philippines, 1971. Blackburn often returned to the Philippines for several state dinners and commemorations honoring the USAFFE guerrillas.*
The Donald D. Blackburn Collection

able people I have ever met. It was truly an honor to meet him and his family. By invitation of his daughter Susan, I had the blessed opportunity to attend Blackburn's funeral at Arlington National Cemetery on November 5, 2008. I am forever indebted to the Blackburn family for their kindness and hospitality.

In a career that spanned over thirty years, Donald D. Blackburn proved himself to be a remarkable leader. As an unwilling transferee to the Philippine Islands, Blackburn refused to surrender even when the Americans' situation looked hopeless. Maintaining his courage and the will to win, Blackburn endured disease, starvation, manhunts, fair-weather friends, and constant brushes with death. Picking up the pieces of a shattered Philippine-American force, he organized a guerrilla regiment that devastated the Japanese in the Cagayan Valley of North Luzon. By the end of the war, his headhunters had killed so many Japanese troops, that the enemy commander swore Blackburn must have had 10,000 guerrillas at his back.

In the opening days of the Vietnam War, Blackburn changed the course of the special operations campaign. Aggressively sending reconnaissance teams into Laos, Blackburn started a program that would eventually interdict over 1,500 tons of enemy hardware and kill thousands of enemy troops infiltrating South Vietnam through the Ho Chi Minh Trail. And although the Son Tay Raid failed to recover any POWs, its tertiary effects were felt throughout North Vietnam. Morale among the American prisoners-of-war surged to an all-time high, and their treatment (including food and medical care) improved significantly.

Having made vital contributions in two of America's greatest conflicts, Donald Dunwoody Blackburn was a true hero of the Army Special Forces.

Blackburn's daughter, Susan, holds up a jacket bearing the words "Blackburn's Headhunters" with the SOG unit crest sewn in the center. This jacket was specially made for Blackburn by a group of SOG veterans. The Donald D. Blackburn Collection

CAREER CHRONOLOGY

DONALD D. BLACKBURN

Born September 14, 1916, West Palm Beach, Florida
Graduated Plant High School, 1934, Tampa, FL
Graduated University of Florida, 1938
Commissioned 2LT, Infantry, US Army Reserve, May 30, 1938
Attended law school, Georgetown University, Washington DC,
    1938–1940
Entered Active Duty, September 22, 1940
Battalion Signals Officer, 24th Infantry Regiment, Fort Benning, GA,
    1940–41
Philippine Campaign:
- Communications and Motor Transport Instructor, Headquarters
    Battalion, 12th Infantry Regiment, Philippine Army, 1941–42
- Division Signal Officer, 11th Division, Philippine Army
- Guerrilla activities in North Luzon, May 1942–August 1945
- Commander, 11th Infantry Regiment ("Blackburn's
    Headhunters"), USAFIP-NL, 1945
Provost Marshal, Military District of Washington, 1946–47
Student Officer, Infantry Officers' Advanced Course, Fort Benning,
    GA, 1947–48
Instructor, U.S. Military Academy at West Point (Dept of Military
    Psychology and Leadership), 1950–53

Armed Forces Staff College, Norfolk, VA, 1953
Plans Directorate, NATO Allied Forces Northern Europe, 1954–56
Commander, 3rd Training Regiment, Fort Jackson, 1956
Senior Advisor, 5th Military Region, MAAG—Vietnam, 1957–1958
Commander, 77th Special Forces Group, 1958–60:
- Operation White Star, Laos, 1959
- Initiates ARVN Ranger training program, creating one of the
  most elite South Vietnamese units in the history of the Vietnam
  War.

National War College, 1960
Deputy Director of Developments for Special Warfare, Office of
  Chief of Research and Development, 1961–64
Director of Special Warfare, Office, Deputy Chief of Staff for
  Operations, 1964–65
Commander, Studies and Observations Group (MACV-SOG), May
  1965–May 1966:
- Discovers the intricate network of the Ho Chi Minh Trail
- Over 40 reconnaissance missions into Laos
- Establishes SOG Forward Operating Bases throughout South
  Vietnam

Assistant Deputy Director, Defense Communications Planning Group,
  August 1966–August 1967
Assistant Division Commander, 82nd Airborne Division, September
  1967–October 1968:
- Deploys the Division's 3rd Brigade to Vietnam.
- Deploys other Division assets to quell the riots in Washington,
  DC.

Director of Plans and Programs, Office of Chief of Research and
  Development, October 1968–1970
Special Assistant for Counterinsurgency and Special Activities
  (SACSA) to the Chairman, Joint Chiefs of Staff, 1970:
- Architect of the Son Tay Prison Raid. Attempt to rescue 55
  American hostages from Son Tay in North Vietnam.

Retired from the Army in July 1971
Vice-president, Braddock, Dunn & McDonald (BDM) Corporation,
  Virginia (military think tank) (retired 1979)
Died May 24, 2008, Sarasota, Florida
Buried in Arlington National Cemetery, Virginia

AWARDS

Silver Star
Legion of Merit with 3 oak leaf clusters
Bronze Star
Purple Heart
Meritorious Service Medal
Air Medal
Army Commendation Medal
Army Reserve Components Achievement Medal
American Defense Service Medal (with bronze service star)
American Campaign Medal
Asiatic-Pacific Campaign Medal (with three service stars)
World War II Victory Medal
Army of Occupation Medal
National Defense Service Medal (with bronze service star)
Armed Forces Expeditionary Service Medal
Vietnam Service Medal (with three service stars)
Armed Forces Reserve Medal
Meritorious Unit Commendation
Philippine Presidential Unit Citation
Philippine Liberation Ribbon
Philippine Independence Medal
Vietnam Campaign Medal
Presidential Unit Citation
Vietnamese Army Distinguished Service Medal
Master Parachutist Badge
Combat Infantryman Badge
Special Forces Tab

BIBLIOGRAPHY

Primary Sources

Blackburn, Donald D. "War within a War: The Philippines 1942–1945," *Conflict*, Volume 7-2, 1988.

Blackburn, Donald D. "Operations of the 11th Infantry. USAFIP-NL (PA) in the Capture of Mayoyao, Mt. Province, Luzon, PI, 26 July–8 August 1945." Capstone research paper submitted by Blackburn for graduation from the Infantry Officers Advanced Course, Class No. 2, 1947–48.

The Donald D. Blackburn Collection.
Various letters, documents, and photographs pertaining to Blackburn's service in the Philippines and Vietnam. Collection was previously stored at Blackburn's residence in Sarasota, Florida. It has since been donated to the Special Warfare History Support Office at Fort Bragg, North Carolina. Highlights of the collection include:

Blackburn's SOG Briefing to General Westmoreland—June 1, 1965.

Blackburn's SOG Files. Various correspondences relating to SOG operations and Reconnaissance Teams, 1965–66.

Certified copy of the document entitled "Confirmation and Record of Orders Issued by Guerrilla Commanders." Document was originally signed by Secretary of the Army Kenneth O. Royall on August 12, 1949.

Loose-leaf binder from the Combat Development & Test Center Vietnam; SPECIAL REPORT; Pictorial Review Vietnam 1963. Binder includes pictures from Saigon and the Mekong Delta.

Anderson, Jack and Dale Van Atta. "Military 'Fiasco' Really a Success." *Washington Post*. July 10, 1985. Article re-evaluating the public's impression of the Son Tay Prison Raid.

Collection of letters to and from Blackburn explaining Volckmann's contributions to Army Special Forces and Volckmann's service under BG Robert A. McClure.

The Mariano D. Manawis Collection.

Mariano Manawis was Blackburn's chief of intelligence during the guerrilla campaign. After the war, Manawis became a celebrated writer in the Philippines, penning such books as *The Fighting Tenth* and *In The Beginning*.

Headquarters, 11th Infantry (S-2). "Summary of Records of the 11th Infantry, PA." Collection of various intelligence reports and narratives, 1944–45.

Headquarters, 11th Infantry (S-2). "Various Materials: Pilots Rescued By 11th Infantry; Adventures of S-2 Agents; Interesting Incidents; Letters to Captain Manawis; Bolomen." Reports and depositions compiled by Mariano Manawis, January–August 1945.

Headquarters, 11th Infantry (S-2). "Enemy Troop Movements: Cagayan, Isabela, Apayao, Bontoc, and Ifugao—February to May 1945."

Headquarters, 11th Infantry (S-2). Compilation of aerial reconnaissance photographs supplied by US Army Air Force to Manawis, 1944–45.

Records of the Adjutant General's Office, Philippine Archives Collection, National Archives II, Record Group 407.

Box 250. Battle Records.

Box 251. Intelligence Reports.

Box 255. "Guerrilla Resistance Movement in the Philippine Islands." Monograph composed by Major General Charles Willoughby.

Box 258. "Volckmann's History," Claude Thorp File, Cagayan-Apayao Forces.

Box 297. Ablan's Guerrillas.

Box 465. General Orders, GHQ, USAFIP, North Luzon. Orders issued periodically from GHQ spanning September 1943–May 1945.

Box 468. More General Orders and Correspondence, USAFIP-NL.

Box 539. Maps of USAFIP, North Luzon Area of Operations, Tables of Organization and Equipment.

U.S. Army Military History Institute. Carlisle Barracks, Pennsylvania. The Donald D. Blackburn Papers.

Blackburn, Donald D; Brigadier General, USA (Ret). Interview by Lieutenant Colonel Robert B. Smith, USAF. Senior Leaders' Oral History Program (Project 83-9). U.S. Army Military History Institute, 1983.

The Russell W. Volckmann Papers.

Box 1. G3 Operations.

Box 4. G3 Operations (cont'd); USAFIP-NL After-Battle Report.

Box 5. Miscellaneous Papers and Maps.

Box 6. G2 Periodic Reports; Intelligence Summaries.

Box 7. G2 Weekly Reports.

U.S. Military Assistance Command, Vietnam, Studies and Observation Group. *Annex A: Command History, 1964.* Saigon: MACV-SOG, 1965.

U.S. Military Assistance Command, Vietnam, Studies and Observation Group. *Annex N: Command History, 1965.* Saigon: MACV-SOG, 1966.

U.S. Military Assistance Command, Vietnam, Studies and Observation Group. *Annex M: Command History, 1966.* Saigon: MACV-SOG, 1967.

Volckmann, Russell W. "Guerrilla Days in North Luzon: A Brief Historical Narrative of a Brilliant Segment of the Resistance Movement during Enemy Occupation of the Philippines 1941– 1945." Camp Spencer, La Union (Philippines): United States Army Forces in the Philippines, 1946.

Secondary Sources

Gargus, John. *The Son Tay Raid: American POWs in Vietnam Were Not Forgotten.* Texas A&M University Press, 2007.

Harkins, Philip. *Blackburn's Headhunters.* New York: WW Norton & Company, 1955.

Meyer, Harold J. *Hanging Sam: A Military Biography of General Samuel T. Williams.* Denton: University of North Texas Press, 1990.

Morton, Louis. *The Fall of the Philippines.* Washington, DC: Office of the Chief of Military History, Department of the Army, 1953.

Norling, Bernard. *The Intrepid Guerrillas of North Luzon.* Lexington: University Press of Kentucky, 1999.

Plaster, John. *SOG: A Photo History of the Secret Wars.* Boulder, Colorado: Paladin Press, 2000.

Plaster, John. *SOG: The Secret Wars of America's Commandos in Vietnam.* New York: Onyx, 1997.

Saal, Harve. *Behind Enemy Lines: MACV-SOG Studies and Observations Group*, Vols. 1–4. Ann Arbor, Michigan: Edwards Brothers Publishing, 1990.

Schemmer, Benjamin. *The Raid: The Son Tay Prison Rescue Mission.* New York: Ballantine Books, 1976.

Smith, Robert Ross. *Triumph in the Philippines.* Washington, DC: Office of the Chief of Military History, Department of the Army, 1963.

Spector, Ronald H. *Advice and Support: The Early Years, 1941–1960* (part of the *US Army in Vietnam* series). Washington DC: Army Center for Military History, 1983.

Thomas, William C. "Operation Kingpin: Success or Failure?" *Joint Forces Quarterly*, Spring 1997.

US Army Special Forces, 1961–1971 (CMH Publication 23-90). Washington, DC: Army Center for Military History, 1989.

INDEX

Kabugao, 109; Kamayong, 86–91, 94–95; Kiangan camp, 78, 83, 93; La Paz, 64; Laos, 156–157; Lapham, Robert, 64–65; Lusod sawmill, 73; MAAG-Vietnam, 142–144, 148, 150, 158–160; malaria, 55, 69–70, 72, 74, 84; Manila, Philippines, 41, 43–44; Manriquez, 103; marries Ann Smith, 131; Mayayao campaign, 124; Mayayao, battle of, 125–127; meets Volckmann, 45–46; "missing in action", 131; Moses and Noble escape from Bataan, 53; Moses and Noble, meeting with, 69, 71; Mount Arayat, 63; move to Manaoag, 29; movement to the Philippines, 20–22; Nagulian, 37–38; National War College, 161; Natividad, 59–60; NATO Planning Group, 179; New Years Day, 1943, 80; news of Japan's surrender, 127–128; news of Pearl Harbor attack, 28–29; Nungawa, 77; Oding camp, 69–70, 72, 74, 76, 92; one-year anniversary of Pearl Harbor, 78; one-year anniversary of surrender at Bataan, 86; Operation *Shining Brass*, 167, 169, 171, 174–176; Operation White Star, 7; "Operations of the 11th Infantry, USAFIP-NL", 10; orders for the Philippines, 19; organize guerrillas in North Luzon, 81–82; Overseas Internal Defense Plan, 183; Philippine

diary, 9, 11; Plans directorate at AFNORTH, 139, 141; *Polar Circle*, 186; POW Reorientation Program, 131, 133; pre-war supply issues, 24–25; promoted to Lt. Colonel, 116; promoted to Colonel, 141; promoted to Brigadier General, 180; Red Floyd, 58; refuses to surrender, 7; rejoins the 11th Division, 43–44; relieves Dumlao, 125; Research and Development branch, 160; retires in Florida, 193; returns to the states, 129, 131; Robert Arnold, 103; ROTC, 15–16; San Juan Line, 32; Senior Advisor, 5th Military Region, 145–148, 150, 159; severed heads, 116; Solana raid, 107–108, 111–112, 115–116, 118; Son Tay Prison Raid, 8, 11, 183–192, 195; Son Tay Raid fallout, 193; Special Assistant to the Chairman for Counterinsurgency and Special Activities, 183, 185; Special Warfare Center, 10, 161; Studies and Observations Group (SOG), 7–9; supplies from the *Gar*, 108–109; *Surrender—Hell!* 10; Thompson Act of 1932, 15; Thorp, 59–62; training troops, 24; troop discipline, 25; troops can't speak English, 26; Tuguegarao, 107, 121; Umingan, 28; units at full strength, 114; University of Florida, 15, 18; US Army Land Warfare Laboratory, 161; Vietnam, 7; Wainwright, 42;